Caught
in the Spell
of Writing and Reading

Grade 3 and Beyond

Margaret E. Mooney
Terrell A. Young

Caught
in the
Spell
of Writing and Reading

Grade 3 and Beyond

Margaret E. Mooney
Terrell A. Young

WITH CONTRIBUTIONS BY
Marsha Riddle Buly
Erin Lucich
Jerry Miller
Brenda Parkes
Mary Ann Whitfield

Richard C. Owen Publishers, Inc.
Katonah, New York

Caught in the Spell of Writing and Reading: Grade 3 and Beyond

Outcomes and Approaches table © 2006 by Margaret E. Mooney

Figure 3.2: Flowchart from *All About Potatoes,* page 16, © 2004 by Newbridge Educational Publishing

Figure 3.3: Diagram from *Ring of Fire* © 2002 by Newbridge Educational Publishing

Figures 3.4 and 3.5 excerpts from *The Memory Coat* text © 1999 by Elvira Woodruff; illustrations © 1999 by Michael Dooling

Figure 3.6: *Exploring Everyday Wonders* © 2000 by Newbridge Educational Publishing

Figure 5.1: The Reading Process © 2005 by Richard C. Owen Publishers, Inc.

Figures 5.7 and 5.11: Record of Learning forms © 2006 by Erin Lucich

Figure 5.8: Record of Learning supporting the reader-writer connection form © 2006 by Erin Lucich

Figure 6.1: Different entry points to planning for writing © 2006 by Margaret E. Mooney

Figure 7.5: Sample conference and track-ing questions for the middle grades form © 2006 by Kim Gasper

Figure 7.6: Simple conference format for beginning of the school year and Figure 7.7: Revised conference format for later in the school year forms © 2006 by Dawn Christiana

Figure 7.8: Examples of teacher's monitor-ing notes on labels © 2006 by Kim Gasper

Figure 7.9: A class chart focusing on the needs of the student form © 2006 by Kim Gasper as adapted from Dawn Christiana

Figure 7.11: A table for tracking conferenc-es during independent reading time forms © 2006 by Marsha Riddle Buly

Figure 8.1: Characteristics of writing development content © 2005 by Margaret E. Mooney

Figure 8.2: Student goal-setting form, Figure 8.4: Teacher's lesson plan, Figure 8.5: Monitoring form for genre/text form, and Figure 8.6: Monitoring form for writing traits forms © 2006 by Mary Ann Whitfield

Figure 8.3: Learning target and success cri-teria content adapted from *Text Forms and Features,* page 27 and © 2001 by Margaret E. Mooney

Library of Congress Cataloging-in-Publication Data

Mooney, Margaret E.
   Caught in the spell of writing and reading : grade 3 and beyond / Margaret E. Mooney, Terrell A. Young ; with contributions by Marsha Riddle Buly ... [et al.].
   p. cm.
   Summary: "Presents teaching reading and writing through demonstration and shared, guided, and independent approaches, includ-ing making links between reading and writing, by a continuum of support, guidance, and reflection across these approaches in the middle and upper grades"—Provided by publisher.
   Includes bibliographical references and index.
   ISBN-13: 978-1-57274-749-4 (pbk.)
   ISBN-10: 1-57274-749-8 (pbk.)
   1. Language arts (Elementary) I. Young, Terrell A.   II. Riddle Buly, Marsha.   III. Title.

LB1576.M66 2006
372.6—dc22

2006005289

Richard C. Owen Publishers, Inc.
PO Box 585
Katonah, NY 10536
914-232-3903; 914-232-3977 fax
www.RCOwen.com

Acquisitions Editor: Darcy H. Bradley
Production Manager: Kathleen A. Martin
Production Assistant/Copy Editor: Amy J. Finney
Designer: Maryland Composition Inc.

Printed in the United States of America

9   8   7   6   5   4   3   2

Contents

Introduction

by Margaret E. Mooney

This book presents the concepts of "to, with, and by" (Mooney 1990) as approaches to teaching from both the reader's and writer's perspectives. It also emphasizes the importance of making the links between reading and writing through intentional instruction across all approaches in the middle and upper grades. This was our intent and challenge as we invited colleagues to contribute chapters to this book. Authors were encouraged to maintain their own writing style, share their experiences, and present their understandings of the practices or approaches to the teaching of reading and writing. Editorial considerations were respectful of the different voices, accepting that this may cause readers to change their reading style and pace as they begin a new chapter. However, it is hoped that readers will enjoy the range of dialogues they can create as they interact with the authors.

While this publication comprises several voices and perspectives, it endeavors to show the interdependence of the approaches and the inextricable links among the various language modes, but especially those between reading and writing. Although each chapter deals with a different approach, and separate chapters focus on reading and on writing, this is purely an organizational strategy to bring a particular section to the fore for detailed discussion. Understanding the intent of each approach and its nature, benefits, and practicalities needs to be considered in the context of the whole that is greater than the sum of its parts. Although four key approaches are addressed in this book, it is acknowledged that other approaches, such as literature circles or reciprocal teaching, make major contributions to a student's development. The labels "to or by, shared, guided, and independent" are umbrella terms and include some of the specific practices promoted through these specific determinants.

The chart in Figure 1 underpins all chapters within the book. It is suggested that readers use this as a reference when commencing a new chapter or when reflecting on the place of any approach within those key to a comprehensive literacy program. The introductory page for each part of this book also provides a quick reminder of the approach in relation to the other three.

	Desired Outcome	Student's Activity and Thinking	Support/Guidance	Teacher's Role	Approach
PART 1	Self-awareness	Observing Listening Absorbing *There is something in this for me. I want to be able to do likewise.*	Support	Modeling and inspiring Showing benefits of a skilled reader/writer in action	Read to or write for
PART 2	Self-correcting	Absorbing and practicing alongside a more knowledge-able other *I want to try to do this. I can practice with someone else.*	Support and guidance	Demonstrating—explicitly explaining—the "how" as well as the "what" to encourage participation	Shared reading/writing
PART 3	Self-assessing	Practicing and applying in other contexts *I can apply what I have learned as I practice by myself with someone watching and guiding me. I can overcome challenges by thinking about what I am learning. The more I practice, the easier it becomes.*	Guidance	Monitoring through interactive formative assessment (nurturing rather than measuring), questioning, provoking, focusing on how meaning is accessed	Guided reading/writing
PART 4	Self-improving	Gaining confidence in applying learning and meeting new challenges in self-selected contexts. *I can use what I have learned in other contexts. I can think about ways I can improve. I can use what I have learned to learn new things.*	Guidance and reflection	Observing, assessing through formal formative and perhaps some summative procedures, measuring effectiveness of learning and application Planning next learning target and learning opportunities	Independent reading/writing

FIGURE 1: Outcomes and approaches

The layout of the chart is intentional and reflects relatively recent changes in my understandings about the teacher's role. My earlier diagrams or explanations differentiating among the approaches usually listed the teaching approach in the left-hand column as the starting point and dominant feature. **The emphasis in this book is that all instruction, practice, application, and much of the assessment should begin with and remain centered on the learner.** The intent and nature of the approach and of the resources must be manipulated to enhance the learner and learning, not the learner or the learning manipulated to "fit" the approach or the resource. The teacher is the stage manager, ensuring that carefully selected resources are presented in a manner that encourages and nurtures learning. So while each chapter focuses on a particular approach, readers are urged to be mindful that very few, if any, lessons will be exclusive to any one approach. Each student's commitment to (and success in) learning will require the teacher to "change gears" and for one approach to slip to another. What began as shared reading may become a guided session for the remainder of the lesson as the students show themselves able to overcome most of the challenges of the reading. In the same way, it is likely that a guided writing lesson will include some independent writing, when each student applies and extends some recently acquired strategies and skills. However, in most cases the amount and nature of the changing support within any one lesson will not cross more than one approach unless the resource or task proves too be far too difficult or offers insufficient challenge or opportunity for extension.

The use of learner-centered words in the first column, "self-awareness," "self-correcting," "self-assessing," and "self-improving," keeps the focus on the expected outcomes for the learner. These words also reflect the sequence of effective learning when what is known through instruction, practice, and application becomes the focus for assessment and the springboard for meeting new challenges. The inclusion of the word "self" is also an important reminder that learning itself is not a gift that we can give students or one that students can receive from anyone else. The gift they can be given is being shown how to learn. Being shown how to learn does not ensure that learning takes place. Each student must actively and thoughtfully engage in the learning. The transition from being shown the product of the learning through to being provided with opportunities to practice and take ownership of the learning underpins the intent of the approaches and of this book.

While reading to and writing for students are supportive approaches with a more knowledgeable other taking the lead by modeling or demonstrating strategies, especially thinking patterns, the learner's role is not one of passive reception. The second column summarizes some of the thinking that effective learning requires as the learner assumes responsibility for exploring and overcoming challenges and becoming comfortable with the new knowledge, understandings, and skills through to being able to apply them in a range of contexts.

The amount and nature of support from the teacher, instructor, or coach changes as the learner assumes responsibility. The third column shows that the learner increases commitment and participates more actively in the learning. The supportive, instructive role gradually changes into one of guidance and then one of reflection as opportunities for increased or new challenges are planned.

The role of the more knowledgeable other as described in the fourth column includes constantly watching for moments when the learner teeters between knowing and not knowing and then knowing at a deeper level or in new areas. Wavering between the known and unknown can cause the learner some discomfort, but the effective teacher is continually watching and listening, ever-ready to provide just enough support and guidance to nudge the student into the unknown without fear of failure or frustration.

The labeling of the approaches provides a quick reference or "shorthand" code. However, it also has the potential to gloss over the importance of ensuring that the student's learning leaves a residue of knowledge, understandings, and skills worthy of the effort expended. Every lesson should include some challenge, for without the "rub" of the unknown, no learning can take place. Ascribing labels to the approaches has led to the creation of definitive definitions of the approaches or sets of exclusive procedures. These can cause teachers to become rigid in their implementation of any one of the approaches. In such cases, the procedures assume more importance than the fundamental premise of this book—the effectiveness of any approach is the degree to which it supports continuous and successful learning and application within and by each student.

The successful selection and adaptation of any instructional approach is dependent on the teacher's understanding of each student's competencies and interests as well as experiences contributing to the learner's perception of him- or herself as a reader or writer. Most students moving into intermediate grades are competent in strategies for basic decoding, comprehension, and composition strategies. However, the greater range of texts, especially those in the more specific content areas, and the expectations of speedier reading and writing of longer and more complex texts present new challenges in all areas of reading and writing development.

Readers who have made steady progress in the early stages come to Grade 3 with an understanding of their role as meaning makers and with an acceptance that their meaning may differ from that of other readers. They understand how the essential rhythm of predicting and confirming and, where necessary, self-correcting enables comprehension to the point of being able to restate what they have read in their own words. Re-reading to increase fluent reading with sufficient pace and expression to maintain a meaningful dialogue with the author will be well established. Their knowledge and use of a wide range of sound and letter patterns, common affixes, and the main word functions will bring sufficient confidence for reading unfamiliar grade level texts to complete assignments as well as texts composed for pleasure. Students working at third grade understand the relationships among their topic, form, audience, and purpose when planning, drafting, and revising their writing. However, as with all strategies and skills mentioned in this section, further development through intentional planned instruction is necessary.

These skills and strategies form a foundation that needs to be nurtured and extended through the same passionate and focused planning, instruction, practice, and assessment that supported the earlier learning experiences. Challenges in the increasing range of texts and higher expectations in exploring and understanding the reader's and the writer's role include the following:

- Understanding the purpose and features of a range of writing forms in order to pursue interests and successfully research and record ideas and information in all curriculum areas

- Integrating decoding and encoding strategies to the point of automaticity in order to attend to deeper levels of understanding than those previously accessed or recorded

- Considering topics, themes, or issues from more than one perspective in order to engage in a more critical dialogue with the author or to provoke the same within the reader

- Exploring and evaluating techniques that capture and sustain a reader's attention

- Maintaining focus when working with several texts, including longer and more complex works in a variety of subjects and styles

- Evaluating the credibility and worth of what has been read or written.

In order to develop competencies to match the increasing demands of reading and writing in the middle and upper grades, some adjustments need to be made to the instruction that was probably delivered in earlier grades. Despite the usual trend to shorten the time devoted to reading and writing instruction in upper grades, more time is actually needed for a session using any one of the approaches. This may mean that fewer groups can meet during a day or only one or two approaches included in any reading and writing lesson. However, it needs to be emphasized that the strategies from any approach are applicable to instruction in all other curriculum areas. "Every classroom teacher has the direct responsibility for developing those reading skills and abilities essential for adequate comprehension within his particular area of instruction, as well as for applying to his content field and make functional those skills and abilities being developed by teachers in other areas of instruction" (Artley 1944, 464).

By the time students reach third grade, and progressively thereafter, those feeling discouraged, confused, or overwhelmed by reading and/or writing or by the expectations put upon them will have developed avoidance tactics. They may become "passengers" within class or group situations, finding excuses to absent themselves from group or one-on-one settings. Engagement from every student in every lesson should be a critical consideration when selecting the approach for any lesson. Some students will have learned how to be the dominant voice in a discussion, justifying their opinions in more detail than necessary, constantly interrupting or ignoring the views of their peers. The role of being a respectful and active group member needs to be included in each of the approaches. This instruction should include ways of eliciting, exploring, and responding to the opinions, concerns, feelings, and experiences of every group member.

Other changes necessary to the way the approaches are planned and implemented at the earlier levels include the selection of resources. Texts used in each of the approaches need to reflect the burgeoning number of topics covered as students progress through the grades and the increasing challenges in writing style, vocabulary, layout, length, form, graphics, concepts, and expected outcomes. Students should not be expected to write in genres or to use techniques that have not been modeled, demonstrated, explained, and practiced in supported and guided lessons. Material used in each of the approaches should reflect that which the students are expected to read and/or write by and for themselves. This means, for instance, that textbooks, including those from content areas, need to be used in read to and write for and shared reading and writing sessions as well as during guided and independent activities.

Whatever approach is selected as the starting point or focus of a lesson, the instruction should reflect the following:

■ Attainable targets and clear success criteria, understood by the learner

■ Formative and summative assessment, identifying achievements and setting new targets

■ Evidence-based practices: explicit modeling, demonstrating, and explaining followed by supervised and supported practice and application and then independent application and extension

■ Material that supports the targets and has relevance for the learners

■ A coordinated sequence of skills and strategies, congruent with state and district requirements

■ Sufficient duration to enable learning to occur without frustration

■ Settings (including small groups) that encourage full and continuous participation from each student

■ Flexibility of pace and grouping to allow for differentiated instruction.

This book seeks to help teachers reflect on their understandings of and practices in developing readers and writers. We do not claim expert status or exclusivity in any way. We are sharing our current understandings in a learning journey that continues to explore new vistas.

PART 1

Casting the Spell

CHAPTER 1
Reading to Students
Terrell A. Young

Terrell Young is a professor of literacy education at Washington State University, where he teaches a variety of undergraduate and graduate courses in children's literature and reading. Terry taught elementary school for twelve years in Wyoming, Utah, and Venezuela. He is the past president of both the Washington Organization for Reading Development and the IRA Children's Literature and Reading Special Interest Group and the current president of the NCTE Children's Literature Assembly. Named IRA's 2006 Teacher Educator of the Year, Terry has written many books and articles on literacy. He is blessed to be married to a wonderful elementary music teacher and to have four terrific kids to remind him of his imperfections.

CHAPTER 2
Writing for and with Students
Margaret E. Mooney

Margaret Mooney is a teacher, writer, and consultant dividing her time between her homeland of New Zealand and the United States. Much of her current work focuses on the interdependence of reading and writing, where one of her mantras is "You learned from an author—now use 'it' as an author." When she is not teaching or writing, her moments are filled with writing (yes, for pleasure), quilting (her latest obsession), and gardening (her obsession until quilting came along).

	Desired Outcome	Student's Activity and Thinking	Support/Guidance	Teacher's Role	Approach
PART 1	Self-awareness	Observing Listening Absorbing *There is something in this for me. I want to be able to do likewise.*	Support	Modeling and inspiring Showing benefits of a skilled reader/writer in action	Read to or write for
PART 2	Self-correcting	Absorbing and practicing alongside a more knowledge-able other *I want to try to do this. I can practice with someone else.*	Support and guidance	Demonstrating–explicitly explaining–the "how" as well as the "what" to encourage participation	Shared reading/writing
PART 3	Self-assessing	Practicing and applying in other contexts *I can apply what I have learned as I practice by myself with someone watching and guiding me. I can overcome challenges by thinking about what I am learning. The more I practice, the easier it becomes.*	Guidance	Monitoring through interactive forma-tive assessment (nurturing rather than measuring), questioning, provok-ing, focusing on how meaning is accessed	Guided reading/writing
PART 4	Self-improving	Gaining confidence in applying learning and meeting new challenges in self-selected contexts. *I can use what I have learned in other contexts. I can think about ways I can improve. I can use what I have learned to learn new things.*	Guidance and reflection	Observing, assess-ing through formal formative and perhaps some sum-mative procedures, measuring effective-ness of learning and application Planning next learn-ing target and learn-ing opportunities	Independent reading/writing

Reading to Students

by Terrell A. Young

CHAPTER 1

P atrick Jones' comment considers many factors that lead to why students struggle in reading. Reading to students addresses many of these issues. Not only does reading to students help them find good reading materials and to develop a love for reading, but it also has a key role in strategy and content area learning. This approach is one of the most effective motivational methods for getting students interested in reading. Yet, its potential offers far more than how teachers often utilize the approach in their classrooms, especially for students beyond Grade 3.

WHAT IS THE READING TO APPROACH?

Reading to students is "a supportive approach where a skilled reader, acting on the author's behalf, reads to a less skilled audience. The ultimate goals are the enjoyment of the ideas and the way they are presented and motivation to savor the benefits of reading for oneself" (Mooney 2004, 73). Teachers who read aloud to their students provide a model of fluent, expressive reading. Moreover, they share their passion for reading and demonstrate reading's many functions: for pleasure, gaining information, meeting personal needs, solving problems, taking an escape, and providing writing road maps. Reading to students plays a fundamental role in "inviting listeners to be readers" (Fisher, Flood, Lap, and Frey 2004, 8).

Many teachers have learned that reading daily to their students is a sound investment of their time. I believe that the daily reading aloud of a poem, picture book, chapter from a chapter book, and "non-book" nonfiction enriches students' lives and provides them with a full range of reading genres and text forms (Cunningham and Allington 2003; Friedberg and Strong 1989; Mooney 2001). "Non-book" nonfiction includes, among other things, newspaper and magazine articles, bus schedules, advertisements, and Internet sources. While all this reading takes time in the busy instructional day, it is time well spent.

"Readers struggle for a variety of reasons, but often it is because they fail to find the 'good book' that allows them to break through to see reading as something of value to their lives" (Jones 2001, 67).

Intentional teachers will decide how often to read to their students based on the students' needs and interests and the teacher's purposes. It is possible that teachers who have one group of students for the entire day can read to them at least once each day. Those teachers who work with more than one group of students obviously have less time to read aloud to their students. Yet, they must not make the mistake in thinking that they do not have time to read to their students. In the now classic *Becoming a Nation of Readers,* the authors synthesized numerous research studies and concluded that "The single most important activity for building the knowledge required for eventual success in reading is reading aloud to children" (Anderson, Hiebert, Scott, and Wilkinson 1985). This statement is as important for eighth graders as it is for first graders. Students **need** daily opportunities to hear books read aloud (even if only for ten or fifteen minutes).

WHY IS THE READ TO APPROACH SO IMPORTANT?

Many teachers tend to read aloud less as students progress through the grades. Yet, countless reasons exist for reading to older students, even at the college level. Research studies contribute support for the critical nature of using this approach in the classroom. Frank Serafini and Cyndi Giorgis present the following scientifically based reasons for reading aloud to students beyond the primary grades. Reading aloud:

- Increases test scores

- Introduces readers to new titles, authors, illustrators, genres, and text structures

- Builds a sense of community

- Provides opportunities for extended discussions

- Is pleasurable

- Connects readers with content area subjects

- Demonstrates response strategies

- Increases readers' interest in independent reading

- Provides access to books that readers may not be able to experience on their own

- Provides demonstrations of oral reading and fluency

- Helps readers understand the connection between reading in school and reading in life

■ Provides demonstrations of quality writing

■ Supports readers' development (Serafini and Giorgis 2003, 8–11).

Yet, we cannot just read aloud to students and expect these things to happen. It is the teacher's **intentional** use of the approach that makes the difference. There are other reasons for reading to students. Today's students need to be exposed to the many cultures in our society and world. Reading to students is often the best approach to meet this goal. Moreover, the approach makes it possible to encourage an understanding of the diverse nature of our society. Today's students need to have opportunities to think about and discuss issues related to gender, class, power, and other issues and roles.

HOW IS THE APPROACH USED WITH OLDER STUDENTS?

Teachers create a **community of readers and writers** when their students share common experiences with literature. Such experiences shape students' future interactions with and responses to the books that they experience in shared, guided, and independent reading. Moreover, these experiences mold students' relationships with one another. As students respond to text, they demonstrate diverse ways of thinking about and responding to it. Members of a community understand and talk about literature in special ways.

Read-aloud experiences help students relate to memorable characters. For instance, students laugh together over Grandma Dowdel's over-the-top adventures in Richard Peck's *A Year Down Yonder* (2000) or *A Long Way from Chicago* (1998). They share their indignation over the treatment of African-Americans in Mildred Taylor's *Roll of Thunder, Hear My Cry* (1976), Chris Crowe's novel *Mississippi Trial, 1955* (2002), or that author's nonfiction account of the same event in *Getting Away with Murder: The True Story of the Emmett Till Case* (Crowe 2003). They may even shed tears as they learn to care deeply for the characters who die as in Cynthia Kadohata's *Kira-Kira* (2004) or Ralph Fletcher's *Fig Pudding* (1995).

They also are amazed to learn that incredible and awesome things happen as their teachers read nonfiction. In Jennifer Armstrong's *Shipwreck at the Bottom of the World,* they learn of Ernest Shackelton and his Antarctic expedition and the conditions endured that winter.

> . . . the temperature can sink to 100 degrees below zero Fahrenheit. Cold air masses sliding down the sides of the glaciers speed up until they become winds of close to 200 miles per hour. When winter descends on

the southern continent, the seas surrounding the land begin to freeze at the terrifying rate of two square miles every minute, until the frozen sea reaches an area of 7 million square miles, about twice the size of the United States. It is truly the most hostile environment this side of the moon. Just imagine yourself stranded in such a place. In 1915, a British crew of twenty-eight men *was* stranded there, with no ship and no way to contact the outside world. They all survived" (Armstrong 1998, 1).

Similarly, Nora Prairie Betz, a sixth-grade teacher, read aloud Robert Burleigh's picture book biography of Admiral Bird, *Black Whiteness* (1998), to her students as part of a unit on extreme climates. They were amazed at the challenges Admiral Bird experienced while spending six months alone in Antarctica. Burleigh's inclusion of quotes from Admiral Bird's journal made the dangers of severe cold even more compelling.

Nonfiction also emphasizes that one person can make a difference. Students are impressed when they learn about how Chiune Sugihara, a Japanese diplomat in Poland, saved the lives of hundreds of Jews at great risk to his own career in Ken Mochizuki's *Passage to Freedom* (1997). Reading to students often leads to more independent reading. Students often want to read other books on the same topics or themes. For example, after experiencing *Passage to Freedom,* students may wish to read independently Alison Gold's *A Special Fate: Chiune Sughihara, Hero of the Holocaust* (2000).

Reading to students enhances **vocabulary development**. For instance, Stahl (1999) notes that sixth graders learned as many words from a single period listening to a teacher read as they would by reading the same material independently. Moreover, this approach especially benefits students with lower vocabulary knowledge and English language learners in building their English vocabularies (Hadaway, Vardell, and Young 2002). English language learners generally have better oral language development than their written language abilities. Thus, they learn more easily through listening than reading and writing. Listening to nonfiction is particularly beneficial because it helps students develop the academic knowledge so important for the content areas. While hearing fiction being read aloud increases students' vocabulary in general, it is nonfiction that helps students develop the content-specific words necessary for success in math, science, and social studies.

Nonfiction authors such as Gail Gibbons and Seymour Simon write picture books on science topics. Reading one of the books or portions of the book aloud prior to the students reading a selection on the same topic provides students with a vocabulary boost. For instance, sixth graders gained "enriched vocabularies" from hearing and discussing *Owls* (Gibbons 2005) prior to reading an article on owl pellets. Later, the students dissected owl pellets. The combined literacy activities with hands-on science have a powerful effect on students' interest and achievement.

Reading aloud provides teachers with a way to weave **cultural diversity** into the school day and the curriculum. For instance, as students read about historical immigration practices in social studies, a teacher can help students make the connection to current immigrants by reading aloud from Don Gallo's edited collection, *First Crossing: Stories about Teen Immigrants* (2005). Such books confront many of the stereotypes regarding immigrants and at the same time help teenagers relate to people of their own age. Reading Diane Hoyt Goldsmith's *Celebrating Ramadan* (2001) can help students better understand why their classmates fast during the day for an entire month.

Teachers often read to students to **build background knowledge** when introducing a new topic of study. Before using a K-W-L chart, the teacher first provides students with background via an informational picture book, excerpt from a chapter book, or even from an Internet site. This reading helps all students enter the topic of study at a higher level because their topical knowledge is accessed and provides a shared beginning point. For example, prior to students reading an article on Leonardo da Vinci, the teacher can read excerpts from either Robert Bird's *Leonardo: Beautiful Dreamer* (2003) or Diane Stanley's *Leonardo da Vinci* (1996) and then ask students to spend 90 seconds writing everything they know about da Vinci. Each student can then contribute as they work together to construct a K-W-L chart.

The approach also allows teachers to **extend knowledge** presented in a textbook or unit of study. In textbooks, people and events are often reduced to a few facts. The teacher may choose to read a page or two of a different text in order to enable students to have a more rounded understanding of a person encountered in a textbook. Excellent books about the presidents include Russell Freedman's *Lincoln: A Photobiography* (1987) and *Franklin Delano Roosevelt* (1990), Kathleen Krull's *Lives of the Presidents: Fame, Shame, and What the Neighbors Thought* (1998), and Albert Marrin's *Old Hickory: Andrew Jackson and the American People* (2004). Or a teacher may want to read from Jerry Stanley's (1992) *Children of the Dust Bowl* to provide a deeper and richer understanding of the Great Depression. After a study of Greek Mythology, students will enjoy hearing Rick Riordan's *The Lightning Thief* (2005). Riordan's fantasy brings the ancient gods to the modern world as Percy Jackson, the protagonist, is sent on a quest to prevent the earth's greatest possible war.

Text books traditionally present only one point of view, so many teachers wish to **help students consider other viewpoints** through reading aloud. For instance, while studying about Lewis and Clark's expedition, a teacher may read Virginia Driving Hawk Sneve's picture book *Bad River Boys: A Meeting of the Lakota Sioux with Lewis and Clark* (2005). The book is a fictional account of the encounter from the point of view of three young Lakota boys. Sneve's story explores the wariness and misunderstanding each side met and the ensuing trouble.

The read to approach is also ideal for **writing demonstrations**. As students move through the grades they are expected to master a number of writing forms. Cyndi Giorgis and Nancy J. Johnson note, "Writers can discover various techniques to tell a story, reveal information, and generate poetry when they pay close attention to the ideas and formats in children's books" (2005, 91). Demonstrations focus on how students can write effectively with voice, good leads, sentence fluency, organization, ideas and content, mechanics, and text features. Fifth-grade teacher Angela Edwards read aloud Jonathan London's *Panther: Shadow of the Swamp* to illustrate exemplary use of word choice in nonfiction to a class of fifth graders. Here are the book's first sentences: "The blinding heat of summer quivers above the swamp. A long, thick tail twitches in the saw grass. A shadow flows. It is a panther" (2000, unpaged). After reading the entire selection, Mrs. Edwards utilized a document projector to allow students to look carefully at the text on each page. Students noted the impact of the strong verbs. Occasionally, Mrs. Edwards had students think of more common but less effective words that London might have used. Jeffrey chimed that "*heat of summer quivers* sounds much better than just writing *heat rises*." Emilee noticed how the sentences of varying lengths gave the book a powerful rhythm.

Teachers also read aloud to share how students' favorite authors get their ideas from their life experiences. For instance, Janet Wong's *You Have to Write* (2002) helps students find writing topics and better understand the writing process. Raewyn Caisley's *Raewyn's Got the Writing Bug* (1997) illustrates how reading both nurtures and nourishes good writing. Author biographies, such as Joseph Bruchac's *Seeing the Circle* (1999) and Laurence Pringle's *Nature! Wild and Wonderful* (1997) helps students see how these authors bring their ideas to life–and print. Esmé Raji Codell's *Sing a Song of Tuna Fish* (2004), based on the author's fifth-grade diary, demonstrates the power of personal narrative that is so important for students who read a steady diet of fantasy and science fiction but never experience success in writing such stories themselves.

Reading to students is the key to **comprehension strategy instruction**. Effective strategy instruction begins with teachers modeling and thinking through the strategy. Teachers generally explain the strategy and how using it helps them become better readers and then share how they use the strategy while reading to students. For instance, teacher Nicole Blake begins reading Allen Say's *Tea with Milk* (1999) aloud, stopping periodically to share what she thinks the story is about. She uses terms such as "I'm thinking . . .," "At first I thought . . . but now I'm thinking . . .," "This is really different than what I thought it was going to be," "Here's what I'm thinking so far . . .," and "Oh! I'm getting it now . . ." Later Mrs. Blake transfers her thoughts to an anchor chart[1] to both illustrate how her thinking evolved and to help her students learn the language of synthesis (based on Miller 2002, 160–161). Mrs. Blake gradually turns more and more responsibility to her students as she reads Andrea U'ren's *Mary Smith* (2003) so her students can share how they synthesize the story. The book explains how people woke up and got to school or work on time before the invention of alarm clocks. Mrs. Blake reads a portion, allows the students to synthesize the book to that point, charts their responses, and then repeats the process until the book is completed.

HOW DO TEACHERS SELECT BOOKS TO READ ALOUD?

Mooney notes that books chosen for this "approach usually [have] more challenges for students than elements that would support their reading" (2004, 78). Some books lure students to revisit them again and again. Wise teachers take great care in selecting books for this approach because "reading to students is comparable to the optimum advertisement for books as incomparable presents" (Mooney 2004, 78). They consider their students' interests, culture, and literature experiences when selecting material to read aloud. Following are some general considerations for text selection:

- Choose books that are good literature

- Select text that you like and enjoy reading aloud

- Decide on text that students would not choose to read on their own

- Pick text that represents a broad range of genres

- With fiction, look for main characters that are at the students' age or older

- Decide on text to which students can relate.

---

[1] *An anchor chart is a tool used by teachers when teaching comprehension strategies in the form of a piece of paper large enough for a group of students to see and read.*

Intentional teachers are not likely to read the same books to their students year after year. Instead, "each book is thoughtfully chosen to support the skills the students are acquiring in their own reading, their own writing, or their own thinking and learning" (Hahn 2002, 3). One year, fourth-grade teacher Deborah Glatt enjoyed reading *Because of Winn-Dixie* (DiCamillo 2001) to her class. Yet, the following year she noticed that many of her students had already read it and felt that it would be a good literature circles[2] book for others. As she conferred with her students, Mrs. Glatt noted that many who had loved *Because of Winn-Dixie* were struggling with *The Tale of Despereaux* (DiCamillo 2003). She decided to read *Despereaux* to her class. The students were able to enjoy the book through her reading, orchestrated discussions, and light dusting of teaching.

It is important for teachers to keep track of the selections they read aloud to their students. Teachers often note the books they read to their students in some type of log. This log enables them to note which genres their students experienced, the balance between male and female protagonists, balance in cultures, which text features were presented, and which authors and illustrators were introduced.

WHAT GUIDELINES SHOULD TEACHERS CONSIDER IN PLANNING THE READING ALOUD EXPERIENCE?

An effective read-aloud experience does not just happen. Teachers must prepare themselves and prepare their students for the experience.

- Practice reading the text until you feel comfortable.

- Establish clear expectations for the read-aloud experience. Some teachers allow students to draw or take notes while listening to the selection, while others do not. Personally, I do not mind the students drawing if their art deepens their response to and understanding of the text.

- Set the tone by sharing your purpose for reading the book and author information, showing the cover and front matter, or using some artifact that relates to the book.

- Read with expression.

---

[2] *In literature circles, small groups of students meet to discuss books in depth. The discussion is guided by their responses to their reading (Schlick Noe and Johnson 1999).*

■ Sit or stand where all can see the reader and book illustrations clearly.

■ Have a purpose for each reading. Purposes range from enjoyment to teaching or practicing skills to introducing genres and writing forms and so on.

Poetry

Few teachers would say they love poetry, which results in its neglect in terms of read-aloud material, yet many students respond positively to poetry. Unfortunately it is poetry's frequent appearance on state assessments that will likely be the rallying cry that compels teachers to read poetry to their students.

Over the years, researchers learned that students relish humorous poems or light verse. They delight in such books as Shel Silverstein's *A Light in the Attic* (1981), Jack Prelutsky's *It's Raining Pigs & Noodles* (2000), and Colin McNaughton's *Wish You Were Here (And I Wasn't)* (2000). These poets' work abounds in parody, ridiculous rhymes, puns, wordplay, and silliness. Such poetry tickles the ears and plants seeds of joy in the heart. Humorous poetry offers a good entry point into the world of verse; reading aloud at least one such poem a day is a worthwhile beginning practice. After marinating students in humorous poems, teachers can introduce their students to some of the other types of poetry.

Many teachers use poetry to launch or support units of study. Poetry anthologies and collections such as Diane Siebert's *Tour America: A Journey through Poems and Arts* (2006), Lee Bennett Hopkins' *My America: A Poetry Atlas of the United States* (2000), Bobbi Katz's *We the People* (2000), and J. Patrick Lewis's *Heroes and She-roes* (2005) and *Monumental Verses* (2005) are ideal for the social studies curriculum. Likewise, Douglas Florian's *Mammalabilia* (2000) and *Insectlopedia* (1998), along with Jane Yolen's *Wild Wings* (2002), fit nicely with nature studies in science. A rich treasure trove of poetry is available for today's teachers to link across the curriculum.

Poetry presents opportunities for students to practice comprehension strategies they are learning. For instance, teachers can share poems from Jack Prelutsky's *If Not for the Cat* (2004), Rebecca Kai Dotlich's *When Riddles Come Rumbling* (2001), or Georgia Heard's *Creatures of Earth, Sea, and Sky* (1992) when teaching inferences. By reading the poem without the benefit of the title or illustrations, the students infer the poems' subjects.

Exposing students to a plethora of poetry motivates many of them to write their own poetry. Paul Janeczko's *A Kick in the Head: An Everyday Guide* to *Poetic Forms* (2005) and Avis Harley's *Fly with Poetry: An ABC of Poetry* (2000) provide students with wonderful models and guidelines for writing numerous poetic forms. Other collections focus on an individual form. For example, see *Cool Melons–Turn to Frogs!* (Gollub 1998) and *Least Things* (Yolen 2003) for haiku or *A Poke in the Eye* (Janeczko 2001) and Joan Bransfield Graham's *Splish Splash* (1994) and *Flicker Flash* (1999) for concrete poetry.

Students benefit from hearing poetry. Nancy L. Hadaway, Sylvia M. Vardell, and Terrell A. Young synthesized recommendations for reading poetry aloud.

- Read the poem with expression and enthusiasm.

- Do not rush the lines; look around the room if possible.

- Read the poem at least twice. Multiple readings encourage students to attend to the language and sounds of the words as well as to the meaning.

- Do not explain the poem or impose adult interpretations or "the critics" on the students.

- Lead a discussion that allows students to share their personal responses to the poem (2001; 2002; 2006).

Such a response may be facilitated by using one or two of these facilitating questions (developed by McClure 1990, 47; see also Franco 2005):

- What did you think?

- What did you like about this poem?

- Does this remind you of anything you know about?

- What is the poet saying?

- Any comments about that?

- Let's discuss what is going on here.

- What about this?

Picture Books

Picture books are a unique marriage of art and text–or a "dual narrative in which both pictures and text work together" to tell a story or to share information (Bishop and Hickman 1992). Their length makes them ideal for reading to students. Books such as Diane Siebert's *Heartland* (1989) provide an inviting introduction to the Great Plains. Meanwhile, books such as *Freedom on the Menu* (Weatherford 2004) and *This School is Not White!* (Rappaport 2005) provoke awareness and rich discussion about issues of civil rights that are now taken for granted by most students.

Nonfiction

Reading aloud, in general, develops oral language proficiency, which has a tremendous impact on eventual success in reading and writing. Reading aloud nonfiction in particular has many benefits. When teachers read nonfiction to their students, they:

■ Draw students into the magic of real world topics that expands knowledge and develops schema for future learning

■ Sensitize students to and help them internalize nonfiction text structures

■ Create wonderful links to fictional and other nonfiction texts, and

■ Provide powerful connections to the curriculum (Moss 2002).

However, reading aloud nonfiction rarely seems to occur. In a survey of 537 elementary teachers regarding read-aloud practices, James Hoffman, Nancy Roser, and Jennifer Battle found that none of the most frequently read books included nonfiction (1993).

Sylvia M. Vardell (2003) and her colleagues (Hadaway, Vardell, and Young 2002) note that there are many ways to read nonfiction aloud to students. Their recommended ways of orally sharing nonfiction, including chapter or excerpt reading, caption reading, modeling the use of reference aids or text features, and cover-to-cover reading, are shared in the following sections.

Chapter/Excerpt Read Alouds

Vardell (2003) notes that many informational books are perfect for sharing orally in "bits and pieces." An example of an excellent work of nonfiction, any chapter of which makes interesting sharing, is Sy Montgomery's *The Man-Eating Tiger of the Sundarbans* (2001). Just reading aloud the first chapter, entitled "The Tiger Is Watching," is a fascinating explanation of how Bengal tigers differ from tigers living elsewhere—they eat people. After hearing the chapter, students often seek out the book to learn more about these fascinating animals.

Books in which each chapter stands alone are also effective for reading to students. *Buffalo Hunt* by Russell Freedman (1988) works well for such reading. "From the Brains to the Tail" illustrates how the Indians wasted nothing when they killed a buffalo, or the chapter "With the Buffalo Gone" shows the effect of the buffalo's destruction on the native people. "Tenements: Shutting Out the Sky" from Deborah Hopkinson's *Shutting Out the Sky* (2003) can help students understand the housing problems that immigrants encountered after their arrivals to the United States.

Collective biographies, where each section deals with one individual, work effectively in chapter read alouds. Russell Freedman's *Indian Chiefs* (1987) is an outstanding example. Read the chapter on Sitting Bull and then make other books about him available to the students. Notable examples include Joseph Bruchac's *A Boy Called Slow: The True Story of a Boy Called Sitting Bull* (1994) and James Lincoln Collier's *The Sitting Bull You Never Knew* (2003).

Caption Read Alouds

Many information books are highly illustrated and include captions. By showing pictures and reading the captions, the students see and hear an overview of the book and are exposed to many interesting facts. For example, try Stephen Kramer's *Hidden Worlds: Looking through a Scientist's Microscope* (2001). Students are shocked to see the photograph that accompanies the caption: "Imagine what it would be like to look into the eyes of a carpet beetle SEM x125" (8). Other amazing photos go along with the following captions: "grains of pollen on a sunflower petal SEM x3,350" (9) and "A cell from a smooth muscle, the type of muscle that moves food through your intestines SEM x930" (13). A teacher's intentional perusal of the captions and photographs often motivates students to read the book independently. Another book that is a popular caption read aloud is Kelly Milner Halls' *Dinosaur Mummies* (2003), with intriguing photos that accompany captions such as "Dinosaur mummies, like this fossilized hadrosaur head, are made of hard material—minerals that take the place of the soft tissue as the animal's body decays" (9).

Other outstanding sources for good captions and exciting illustrations include Sally Ride and Tam O'Shaughnessy's *The Mystery of Mars* (1999), Charlotte Wilcox's *Mummies and Their Mysteries* (1993), or Jim Murphy's *The Great Fire* (1995). Reading and sharing captions and illustrations provide an excellent way to incorporate nonfiction into the curriculum and can lead to identifying main ideas (Hadaway, Vardell, and Young 2002).

Introducing Reference Aids and Expository Text Features

Through the reading to approach, it is possible for teachers to introduce or highlight the technical aspects of nonfiction text (Hadaway, Vardell and Young 2002; Moss 2006). This includes the internal text structure for how the author organized the information, such as using chronological sequence, cause and effect, comparing and contrasting, or presenting ideas from the general to the specific. In addition, teachers can model how nonfiction authors use reference aids to help readers access information from the text. These reference aids, text features, or access features, as they are often called, include maps, table of contents, indexes, and glossaries. How the text is organized, with headings and subheadings, boxes and sidebars, and the placement of illustrations and graphic aids such as charts, graphs, and timelines are other aspects of text format that teacher can model (Mooney 2001). Such modeling reinforces needed skills and lays the groundwork for academic study skills.

For example, Dorothy Hinshaw Patent's *Animals on the Trail with Lewis and Clark* (2002) can be used to model how to use a table of contents or an index. Likewise, Diane Swanson's *Safari beneath the Sea* (1994) is a great resource for showing students how authors use sidebars. Sandra Markle's *Outside and Inside Mummies* (2005) works well for teaching the "compare and contrast" text structure. The teacher can highlight the signal words associated with compare and contrast structure. These signal words may include *same as, alike, similar to, resembles, compared to, different from, unlike, but,* and *yet.*

Typically teachers will read narrative nonfiction from cover to cover. Other books to consider reading from start to finish include those books without indexes or contents pages and informational or biographical picture books.

Cover-to-Cover Read Alouds

WHAT ROLE DOES RESPONSE PLAY IN THE READING ALOUD EXPERIENCE?

The purpose of response is not to test student understanding of text. Serafini and Giorgis note that response, instead, should promote reader engagement, deepen students' understanding and appreciation of the text, and help them

> become more sophisticated in their ability to understand and respond to literature, to provide multiple points of entry, and to allow *all* our students to understand and be successful regardless of their prior experiences with literature. The experiences we create should extend students' thinking, support them in adopting multiple view points, include multiple ways of knowing, make connections to other elements of the curriculum, and strengthen their engagement with text (2003, 50).

Conversations, writing, drama, and rituals hold the potential to help readers develop the skills and strategies they need to become better readers. However, it often takes time and patience before these practices bear fruit because they are often unfamiliar to students (Sibberson and Szymusiak 2003).

Douglas Fisher and his colleagues noted that expert teachers consistently use book conversations before, during, and after read-aloud experiences. While such conversations are facilitated by a teacher, students are provided

Conversation

with opportunities "to share their thoughts, reactions, expectations, predictions, or concerns about the book the teacher was reading" (Fisher et al. 2004, 13).

Drama

Joan Parker Webster (n.d.) recommends using **tableau vivant** in response to text. Tableau vivant involves a group of students choosing a portion of text to represent in a frozen scene, as in a painting or photograph. Participants try to convey emotion through their facial expressions and frozen gestures while a narrator tells or reads about the scene. The audience can then question students about their intentions and gestures in the image. Webster also suggests reconstructing the events to create an alternative to what happened in the text.

Another dramatic response to a read aloud is **hot seat**. One teacher utilized this technique after reading the final chapter of Lois Lowry's *The Giver* (1993). In groups of four, the students came up with two questions they would ask Jonas, his mother and father, and the Giver if those characters were present. Next, the teacher invited students to take on those roles. The selected students' responses to questions had to stay in the context of the book and reflect the values of the dystopian society. As a management tool, the students were informed that no "character" could be asked another question until each character had received a question during that round. The students noted that both the questions posed and the responses given added to and strengthened their individual interpretations.

Marcie Belgard's students respond to books through **imagined conversation**. This strategy involves students creating an imagined conversation between book characters or the students themselves and book characters. Students, working in pairs, observe the following guidelines:

- Create two-page written dialogues that will be two to three minutes long when performed before their classmates

- Conversations must remain true to the portrayed characters

- No new characters can be introduced through the conversations.

Students are given a specific amount of time for writing and rehearsing their conversations. The imagined conversations are shared with two or three other groups, and the teacher selects a few to be shared with the entire group.

Writing

Writing is often a good tool for deepening students' thoughts about text. Moreover, the writing is rich fodder for conversation when students share their written responses to text. Teachers can provide students with a prompt or focus their writing on target strategies such as inferring or synthesizing or they may invite them to share their thoughts in writing. For example, at the end of listening to a chapter of *Because of Winn Dixie*, Corey wrote the following response:

I know it is sad, but I think Winn Dixie is gone for good. He helped Opal make friends and learn to talk to her dad, and now he is going off to help some other child that needs him more.

Such responses lay a foundation for more sophisticated reading. Moreover, such writing demonstrates comprehension and prepares students for the written response required in high-stakes exams. Teachers need to be careful not to overdo written responses so that students never think of writing as a "punishment" for reading. Regie Routman suggests that written response to reading take no more than 20% of the time spent reading (2003, 54).

Rituals

In *Reconsidering Read-Aloud,* Mary Lee Hahn (2002) shares read-aloud rituals she applies with her fourth- and fifth-grade students. The rituals include read-aloud gallery, lingering, and the birthday read-aloud.

For her **read-aloud gallery,** Hahn involves her students in creating a visual reminder of a recently completed book. She draws a student's name from a bucket and the student then draws a picture illustrating her or his favorite part of the book. The illustration (along with a sentence strip with the book title and author) is hung in the classroom. This visual reminder of the books creates a chronology of books experienced and a reference point as students make connections from text to text throughout the year (Hahn 2002, 38–40).

Sometimes students are not ready to move on to another book. The **lingering** ritual allows them time to remain under the influence of a book's magic. Hahn noted that re-reading the ending of Sharon Creech's *Walk Two Moons* (1994) a couple of times invited healthy conversation and enabled students "to weave the loose ends of story strands into a final tapestry." The students better understood the book and had more opportunities to talk, laugh, and cry about a book they experienced together (Hahn 2002, 43–44).

A third ritual is the **birthday read-aloud,** when students choose a portion of a book to re-read for their birthdays. Hahn and the classmates enjoy learning about the portion of a book that impressed or affected the birthday student the most. Sometimes these favorites divulge a place where the plot turns, reveal a moral dilemma, or detail the parts of the book that are particularly happy, funny, or sad. These "revisits" often uncover new thinking about the books or share a "rich and complex glimpse into the reader's mind" (Hahn 2002, 40–43).

WHAT STRATEGIES RELATED TO READING ALOUD PROMOTE READING IN THE CLASSROOM?

Time simply does not allow teachers to read every book they want to read to their students, nor every book their students would benefit from hearing. Book talks and readers theatre also promote reading in the classroom.

Book Talks

One of the most effective ways of promoting reading is through "book talks" (Akerson and Young 2004; Allington 2006). In a book talk, the teacher briefly summarizes or reads a portion of a book aloud to get students excited about the selection. For example, *The Snake Scientist* (Montgomery 1999) is ideal for a book talk for intermediate grade students because it shows how a person's passion for nature can lead to a career in science. Moreover, the author's passion for the topic is obvious. The teacher might share some of this book's illustrations and briefly tell about the snakes and the scientist's line of research.

Teachers should regularly present book talks and spend no more than two minutes per book, but share no more than five books at a given time. In this way, students will be exposed to many books over the course of the year. Moreover, having these books in the classroom library makes them much more accessible and thus more likely to be read by the students.

The teacher's purpose for presenting the books will determine which books will be shared. For instance, the teacher may share two fiction books, two nonfiction books, and one poetry book at one time. For literature or idea circles, the teacher shares the students' book choices. Book talks to support a unit would include books related to the theme or topic of study.

Readers Theatre

Teachers find that hearing a readers theatre script based on a portion of a book often motivates students to read the book in its entirety. Teachers can capitalize on the motivational nature of readers theatre by having students prepare and perform readers theatre scripts on books or texts available in the classroom. Readers theatre is frequently considered for fiction, but nonfiction readers theatre scripts highlight books that boys often prefer to read and can support the curriculum (Young and Vardell 1993).

Teachers can find readers theatre scripts online or in teacher resource books, or they can develop their own using the following criteria:

1) Choose an interesting section of text containing the desired content for your purpose. This brief selection should be a teaser with just enough text to encourage students to read the book on their own.

2) Reproduce the text.

3) Delete lines not critical to the section being emphasized, including those that indicate that a character is speaking.

4) Decide how to divide the parts for the readers. Dialogue can be assigned to appropriate characters. With some texts, it will be necessary to rewrite text as dialogue or with multiple narrators. Changing a third-person point of view to a first person (I or we) point of view can create effective narration.

5) Add a prologue to the script in "story-like" fashion to introduce the script and readers. If needed, a postscript can be added to bring closure to the reading.

6) Label the readers' parts by placing each character's name or narrator number in the left-hand margin, followed by a colon.

7) When the script is finished, ask others to read it aloud. Listening to the script may make it easier to make appropriate revisions (adapted from Young and Vardell 1993).

Involving students in creating readers theatre scripts is an excellent way for them to develop critical thinking skills, work cooperatively, and engage in the processes of editing and revision. Readers theatre holds great potential for exposing students to both content and appealing literature.

DEVELOPING LIFE-LONG LEARNING

In conclusion, reading to students is essential for developing students who know how to read and choose to do so. By reading to their students, teachers can model comprehension and book choice strategies while sharing their passion for reading and text. Reading aloud enables students to navigate their way through a variety of genres, text types, and forms and features. Students enjoy this pleasurable activity while developing the skills, stamina, and attributes necessary for life-long learning.

Writing for and with Students

by Margaret E. Mooney

CHAPTER **2**

Writing for and with students in the early school years provides opportunities for the teacher to spark interest in the act of writing and to model some of the ways we record events, ideas, and information through writing. The ensuing attitudes and understandings are then demonstrated and practiced, enabling the students to develop basic competencies as they engage in frequent and meaningful writing experiences.

Writing for students requires us to "walk the talk." Our efforts may falter, and our creations might be less than perfect, but they enable our students to see us as writers rather than just as teachers of writing. And as we write for our students we are reminded of the realities of creating and sharing some of our ideas through the written word.

> T: *Most journal entries are for ourselves, but we have talked about how sometimes we feel our journal jottings are worthy of sharing for the discussion they could engender. As I was writing these notes last night I did have you in mind as a possible audience. I felt that my written words might create a clearer picture than if I only talked about my day at Tiritiri.* (Teacher reads from journal)

Sunday

A great day! One to remember and remember I shall! A, E, and I went to Tiritiri Matangi, the bird sanctuary on Tiritiri Island. Although only 3 miles off shore it's a world apart–a predator-free haven for endangered birds (whose singing let us know it is their territory and we were but guests) and a nurturing nursery for the 280,000 trees volunteers have planted in the last

---

T: *First and foremost, I wanted you to know a little about Tiritiri because I was excited about my day. Secondly, because I wanted to share that with you, I actually did think of my audience (you) as I wrote, and I found that did make me revise my writing more than I would normally do when writing in my journal. And now, thirdly, reading it to you was not as easy as I thought.*

ESSENTIAL ELEMENTS FOR EFFECTIVE WRITING

Motivation and **increasing** competence continue to be essential elements of writing "for and with" lessons for students beyond the first three years of school. However, the lessons also need to model how flexibility and commitment are of increasing importance as both the functional and pleasurable aspects of writing are pursued. Although the four elements of motivation, competence, flexibility, and commitment are interdependent, each will be considered in the context of the "writing for" approach in the first section of this chapter. The second part of the chapter explores how these elements combine and are inherent when writing with students in shared writing.

Seeing a More Knowledge-able Other at Work Increases Motivation

During recent years I have "caught the magic" of quilting. I was (and still am when I can squeeze quilting in for a short while) an embroiderer, so I did not think learning another textile craft would be a challenge. I attended quilting exhibitions and was inspired enough to try my hand at piecing material shapes together in a rather basic pattern. However, after several attempts and increasing frustration, I realized that thinking I could "go it alone" would not work. I joined a small informal group, watched experienced quilters, asked a myriad of questions, and became so inspired that housework and writing went out the door as I set about making another attempt at some simple piecing.

The group meets every two weeks, and I was the first to arrive at that next gathering. The group members enthused about my efforts, recalled their efforts at a similar stage in their journey, and invited me to watch as they continued their work. As we worked–the novice sewing regular-shaped pieces into my second sample block and the experienced working on their intricate designs–the discussion and exchange of ideas and tips raised my expectations of what I could do and gave me sufficient confidence to increase the challenges I put in front of myself. My goals became clearer, and I had examples of the way to work toward those goals. I was able to listen and absorb as I observed experienced quilters at work. The exhibitions had inspired me, but seeing master quilters at work had motivated me to the point of convincing me that quilting was something I could do successfully.

Seeing skilled writers working at their craft is different from seeing a finished text. Our students may be inspired by the writing we choose to read to them or by the writing from our pen we give them opportunity to enjoy, but in order for them to be convinced of the benefits of reading and of their competence as writers, they need to see us crafting texts for them. They need to see the act of writing, and we need to walk the paths they will walk. We need to experience the agonies and ecstasies of composing, editing, revising, and sharing a text within the same parameters that they will encounter in their writing. And the models we create through writing for our students need to be evaluated in the same way as we evaluate their work. Therefore, we need to make our work and other books and authors' work accessible as models for the students' reference. Seeing the work planned and composed will give them greater understanding of the piece than if it had been composed "out of the situation" and then shared with them. Motivation cannot be done through remote control. Their increased understanding will enable them to consider the work more knowledgeably and use it as a measure for their own writing—and it may provide us with some valuable insights into how students feel when their work is shared and critiqued.

Basic Competencies Are a Springboard for Further Development

By third grade, most students have developed basic competencies in writing some fiction and nonfiction texts. They understand, at least at a rudimentary level, the writing process, editing and revising their work according to its purpose and audience. But the curriculum demands of third and subsequent grades require an increased number of texts of increasing complexity, in a wider range of forms, executed in a timely manner, often with more than one text being worked on at any one time. At the same time, accuracy of spelling, grammar, and punctuation conventions and presentation of work assume greater importance—at least in the view of many teachers, although this is often an unconscious assessment criterion. Students need to see how such texts are created and effort sustained. They need to see how what is known and secure in terms of execution can form the springboard for new learning and how practice increases fluency and subsequently competence. The elements of rate, pace, and expression are often considered only in terms of reading, yet they are as critical to developing competence in writing.

Once basic competencies are in place, students are able to take more responsibility for increasing their confidence and skill as writers. Through the "writing for" approach, teachers are able to model how writers set goals (currently labeled as learning targets) and develop rubrics or success criteria, which serve as evaluative stepping stones during and after the writing. Observing how writers set their own targets and evaluative frameworks transforms the motivating desire to write into a clear path, providing supports for the "how" of the composition, and allowing attention to be given to the "what." The support from the learning target and success criteria also shows students how the self-awareness that initially motivates a writer becomes a self-correcting and self-assessing scaffold.

Flexibility in Learning in One Curriculum Area Supports Other Learning

As the students increase their competence in a skill or strategy, the teacher can use the writing for approach to model the use and effectiveness of the new learning in a range of contexts and for an increasing variety of purposes and audiences. For instance, once the students have composed narrative texts practicing the use of comparison to heighten the reader's perception of a character, the teacher can use a series of writing for sessions to model wider use of the technique, emphasizing how learning in one area transfers at least in part to another. Learning about character development when writing narratives forms an effective foundation for reading and writing biographies or texts describing the influence of individuals in contemporary and past civic and national activities. A subsequent session might show how comparison of a protagonist and an antagonist often underpins the plot of a play or a crime novel. Or the focus could be on the difference between using comparison when the characters are known to the probable reader or when one or both are unfamiliar. The difference may be as simple as using more metaphors to speed the reading when characters are known and using more similes when the characters are unknown in order to cause the reader to slow down and ponder a little. Such small, though significant, details need to be modeled before students can be expected to use them appropriately in their own writing. Further sessions could model the use of comparison when establishing the mood or scene of a piece or describing a place in a geography assignment.

It is also critical that writing for sessions show how learning within a class setting can be practiced and explored when writing for oneself. The importance of developing writers who choose to write cannot be emphasized enough, but the business of the classroom and the ever-bulging curriculum often precludes sufficient attention to helping students discover the benefits of writing for, about, and by themselves.

Another important dimension of flexibility that needs to be modeled frequently is how to "twist the pen" in order to cope with the nuances of writing in the various subjects. Within one day, this might include completing assignments and/or taking notes in at least four different curriculum areas and working on assignments for these and other subjects after school hours. Modeled lessons should show the commonalities and differences within the same genre in different subject areas as well as within one curriculum program. For instance, students need to see a skilled writer crafting a book report and how that same writer uses what is known about reports to compose a report of a science experiment. Similarly, students need to see how a writer twists the pen when writing a report about a movie, a poem, or a magazine article.

It is vital that lessons are devoted to showing how experience and culture influence writing styles and perspectives. By the time students leave eighth grade, each will have developed an individual style. However, not only should that style be able to be adapted to a range of contexts, but there should be an understanding of how to consider, evaluate, and learn from texts written from other perspectives. Establishing a community of writers who value, respect, and support the work of others is one of the many important benefits of writing for students.

Flexibility or the ability to use writing for an ever-increasing range of demands and desires is a critical component of motivating and developing successful and enthusiastic writers in the middle and upper grades. It is essential that they do not see writing as a selection of a formula or working to a rubric selected from a predetermined selection, but as a craft where thought and commitment bring rewards and satisfaction.

As students progress through the grades, they are required to sustain effort and interest over a range of subjects and produce longer and more varied and detailed texts. However, the students and teachers are faced with many challenges. These include:

Sustaining Effort and Interest Requires Commitment to the Task at Hand

- The discrete nature of the periods within a school day that often disrupt the flow of writing

- The amount of content knowledge to be acquired, processed, and recorded

- The number of assignments requiring extended or varied responses

- The amount of writing required to be composed or completed beyond the school day, and

- In some cases, the number of teachers setting and assessing assignments, each with his or her own criteria.

Therefore, components of writing for sessions should include attention to how authors manage to maintain effort and interest when working on more than one manuscript at a time, techniques they use to return to a piece from time to time, and how they persevere to complete tasks. The combination of these components is a reflection of a lively self-improving system that is ultimately the aim of all instruction.

When students have frequent opportunities to see their teacher as a motivated and committed writer, able to craft a range of texts and willing to share their writing journey, the act of writing gains huge credibility, attracting a commitment from the students to pick up the pen and do likewise. When we write for students we show that we have walked the same path they are taking, we know whether our demands and standards are reasonable, and we are giving the strongest possible invitation for them to participate in the more supported shared writing session. We can then turn the "I will show you what it is like to write this text at this time about this topic for this purpose and audience" into "I will show you how to do it. Put on your 'in your head' pen and write with me."

The writing spell has been cast. The remainder of this chapter shows how the spell can be nurtured to a fullness of its own accord through writing with students or shared writing. Readers may wonder why shared writing appears to receive greater attention in this book than the other approaches. It is emphasized that all are of equal importance and are interdependent. However, shared writing has recently come under scrutiny because of the many "versions" in the instructional literature and because many teachers of students beyond Grade 3 have asked for support in implementing the approach.

WRITING WITH STUDENTS

For some years I understood the term "shared writing" to denote times when the teacher shared a piece of writing with the students, talking about the strengths and weaknesses, the author, and other pieces by the same author or by different authors dealing with the same topic. At this time, I did not see the teacher as the essential author, demonstrating the act of writing. Later I understood shared writing to be the teacher and students (usually the class) working together to record a common experience with some attention given to sentence construction, word choice, spelling, and punctuation. The students contributed words, spotted inaccuracies, and read the finished piece, which was usually completed at a reasonably fast pace–though not quick enough for the "passenger" students, who had found it more interesting to disturb those around them than to contribute. The purpose was collaboration and the experience was not really considered to be an instructional approach.

I still consider collaborative writing as described above as having a place within a student's writing development. However, I now believe that the shared writing that should assume the greater part of the shared approach and the one I want to discuss in this chapter is more consistent with the explicit demonstrations listed in the chart of instructional approaches on the second page of Part 1 of this book. This approach to shared writing requires the teacher to take the student into a skilled writer's thinking, overtly explaining how ideas are formed, shaped, recorded, and refined. There is no formula for these demonstrations—they will be as varied as the topic, learning target, learner's competence, and the teacher's confidence and skill in sharing his or her writing expertise.

The demonstrations show:

- The range and depth of thinking required to initiate and sustain commitment to a piece of writing, including work requiring more than one session

- The difference between independent writing for oneself, as in a diary or journal, and writing for a specific target, whether it be for an audience, competence in a particular skill or genre, or for a particular function

- How to set a target and success criteria to maintain self-improving development

- How the transfer of learning and skills from one language mode (especially from reading to writing) or subject area to another provides support for learning and application in another

- The individual role and the integration of prewriting, drafting, revision, and proofreading within the act of composing and recording

- How writers overcome challenges, and how and when to seek help or use other resources

- The intrinsic rewards from the act of writing

- Ways a writer works to develop and employ an individual style and voice

- How to think about sharing writing through publishing or presenting

- How to seek and consider feedback from writing partners, more knowledgeable writers, and one's audience

- How to give effective feedback to other writers

Explicit Demonstrations and Explanations Are Essential to Shared Writing

- How writers decide what needs to be recorded in writing for short-term or long-term reference

- How writers use writing to think deeply about what they have read.

The central and common ingredient for any shared writing lesson is that the rehearsal and refinement that precedes and is inherent in any recording is shared and explained in a way that each student can internalize, emulate, and practice until it becomes part of the learner's repertoire. This means that texts written during a shared session should reflect required standards and be attainable, after practice, by most of the students. The focus of shared lessons should be consistent with skills and understandings that the students will be taking responsibility for applying and practicing during guided writing sessions. For example, a shared lesson might explore techniques an author uses to develop characters in a narrative. The students can apply this learning when contrasting two characters in a subsequent piece of writing. The main difference between a shared lesson and a guided one is the balance of the nature and amount of support or guidance and student responsibility.

The Teacher's Role in Shared Writing Is to Make the Act of Writing Accessible to Every Student

The effectiveness of any lesson is dependent on the teacher's knowledge and understanding of the experiences, interest, and competencies that each student brings and the relationship of these to the planned or required curriculum. Some shared lessons can be based on common weaknesses in student work or challenges causing students to be confused or overwhelmed. While these are worthy "teachable moments," another key role of the teacher is to ensure that during the year the demonstrations will cover the gamut of skills designated in the non-negotiable documents of the school or state. An essential tenet when planning shared lessons is that students should only be expected to write in a form or use a skill or technique that the teacher has demonstrated and explained in the composition of relevant examples. So the planning of shared writing sessions needs to be linked to those using the guided approach and also to shared reading, enabling students to have access to examples of other authors using similar techniques or presenting ideas and information in a similar form or style.

In Shared Writing the Teacher "Talks Through" How a Text Is Composed and Refined

The purpose of writing for students is to cause them to want to do likewise. The first task a teacher must accomplish during a shared lesson is to build on that motivation, convincing each student that composing a text of similar quality is achievable. This means that the explanations accompanying the actual writing need to be in sufficient detail and at a level commensurate with the student's understanding to motivate the learner to participate in and sometimes contribute to the composition. This participation may be mainly in the head, predicting, confirming, and self-correcting within the structure or scaffold the teacher presents as she "talks through" how the text is shaped and refined. As the lesson progresses, the teacher needs to change some of the explanations into questions, not expecting every one to be answered audibly, but causing a deeper level of engagement from the students. The students' contributions are accepted and, when appropriate, incorporated into the text, without interrupting the flow of the writing. The students' contributions to the group work are not acknowledged individually or "in the moment" the same way that each student's efforts are during guided reading. However, once the focus of the lesson has been achieved, there should be discussion confirming the contributions, with recognition of how these enhanced the piece. This difference between acknowledgement in shared and guided sessions recognizes the difference between being a partner and being responsible for the creation of the text.

It is usual for the pace of a shared lesson to increase as the students become more engaged and place themselves more consistently in the author's role, but it is important that the teacher does not stop the explanatory role. Many students are challenged by sustaining effort or knowing how to conclude a piece of writing. An important part of every shared lesson should be reflecting on the composition of a satisfactory ending as well as on the product of the lesson and the act of writing—what challenges were overcome, what considerations shaped the writing, and what subsequent learning or action would be prudent.

All shared lessons can be to no avail unless the teacher helps the students understand the intended focus of the lesson and their role of watching, listening, thinking, approximating, self-correcting, and practicing in order to be able to apply the new learning in less supported situations. Essential to this is honesty between teacher and student, with the students comfortable in questioning the teacher's thinking and decisions as they seek to assume their role as thoughtful and intentional learners.

The Students' Role in Shared Writing Is to Practice Alongside a More Knowledgeable Author

In a shared lesson, the students are able to participate in a more taciturn manner than the consistently active and audible role they need to assume in a guided lesson. However, that does not mean they should be passive observers. Students should understand and accept their role of thinking along with a skilled writer, using the more knowledgeable author's explanations and writing as a base for shaping and refining ideas or information and anticipating how it could be recorded. They are using the teacher's thinking, explanations, and recording as a scaffold for their "in the head" composing and editing, with more active and audible participation when they feel their suggestion could make a worthwhile contribution to the piece. Their engagement needs to be a rhythm of watching and questioning and then practicing alongside the model, of absorbing and trying out for oneself, of "I can see how to think about/do this" and "I can try it for myself." This to-ing and fro-ing of suggesting and absorbing, with each student at times the eager contributor and at other times the observant listener, can make for a lively communal session. But each student must know that the main focus must be always on learning—and that each individual must take responsibility for this.

The Pattern of a Shared Writing Lesson Should Provide a Structure that Students Can Use in Their Independent Writing

A shared writing lesson should establish a pattern that will be developed further in guided sessions and that students can replicate independently. Although the writing process is sometimes presented as a one-off sequence of prewriting, drafting, revising, editing, and publishing, most writers find any one piece of writing is a continuous interwoven cycle of the first four. The writer's interest and understanding of the topic and purpose and competence in recording in the appropriate form and style will cause the rhythm to change from piece to piece. And, within any one piece, the ebb and flow will change, with some sections or ideas proving more challenging or requiring more emphasis than others. As with any writing, students participating in a shared session should have a clear understanding of the intention of the writing and the target and outcome of the learning, and the composition section should be followed by reflective discussion and confirmation of the intrinsic rewards of writing.

The Foundations of Writing Have Been Established in the Early Grades

Students entering third grade will have had many shared writing experiences, and although they will have a range of competencies in writing, most will be well prepared for coping with the increased challenges of the middle and upper grades. The majority will have a well-established understanding of:

- The process of initiating and working on a piece of written text to publication stage

- Revision and proofreading being essential to writing, although some may see this as distinct stages after drafting

- The importance of matching sounds in words to letter patterns when recording ideas and information

- The shape of a story, especially beginning, middle, and end, and a problem/solution structure

- The purpose and nature of a basic expository text

- Ways in which the intended purpose or audience influences the shape and focus of the text and the writing process

■ Writing as a common way to respond to what has been read

■ Some of the similarities between reading and writing

■ Each writer having a particular style and voice that distinguishes his or her work from others.

As students progress into and beyond Grade 3, writing becomes more individual and varied. The demands of more definitive, content-oriented learning assessed through assignments and projects bring an increased emphasis on writing to perform. The emphasis expands in breadth and depth through the grades beyond third, so the intentionality of instruction common in the early grades needs to be replicated and increased through the middle and upper grades.

The expansive curriculum of third grade and beyond requires students to be more adept in writing for an increased range of purposes and audiences, to be more resourceful when writing, and to expend effort in developing their own skills and style in order to write confidently and competently. One week's writing could require a seventh-grade student to distinguish between the real and the possible, a theme and an issue, persuasive and unbiased information, a conclusion and a generalization, a general and a narrow perspective, and a structure showing cause and effect and one based on problem and solution as well as understand the difference between writing when assessment will focus on technique and on content and between composing a text of restricted length and one of indeterminate length. And, added to these complexities, the student is required to switch thinking from science to social studies to mathematics and so on. Such complexities cannot be left to osmosis learning–each nuance requires the intentional and focused demonstration and supported practice that shared writing offers. This means that the focus of shared sessions will be more specific and will often be devoted to the why, when, and how of a particular technique or part of the writing process.

The specific nature of content and nature of writing as students progress through the grades requires close engagement with and during the composition and shaping of text. While working with the class may be expedient on some occasions, many of the shared sessions would be of greater benefit when the range of learners is accommodated in some small-group sessions. Shared writing is an instructional approach, worthy of the same considerations as given to the guided approach. A smaller group often allows for a shorter and more focused modus operandi. Whatever organization is implemented, students should see the supportive instruction provided in shared sessions as a vital and regular part of their learning.

Writers in Grade 3 and Beyond Twist Their Pens in Many Directions

Grouping for Shared Writing

Assessment of and for Writing Sustains an Effective Program

Determining the effectiveness of shared lessons has several dimensions. The most obvious may be the degree to which students are able to incorporate their new understandings into their writing in less supported situations, especially in guided and independent contexts. But such a definitive stance may give a false view because new learning from shared lessons receives further support and guidance during guided sessions. Much of the student participation has been "in the head," at times unable to be observed. No one student has been responsible for the text, so it should not be included in any evaluation of the learner. A more realistic assessment may be more attitudinal during and following the shared session, measured by the engagement each student displays during the lesson, the degree to which each contributes to the collaborative writing, and the eagerness to practice independently.

Demonstrating How to Assess One's Writing is Crucial

It is important that a major focus of shared writing sessions should be both of and by the teacher. Some of this focus will be within the teacher and kept close to the chest. However, a crucial part of every shared lesson should be the teacher's honest appraisal of the thinking he or she required and the decisions he or she made during each stage from prewriting through to the completed piece. This evaluation should explain how the students' contribution influenced the teacher's thoughts and decisions, and this evaluation should include feelings as well as the actual content of the contribution and resulting additions or changes. The appraisal should also include discussion of the challenges encountered and how these were overcome as well as which sections were easy or engendered refreshed enthusiasm, allowing the writing to get back on track. Assessment of these aspects shows students how to develop an awareness of their own strengths and weaknesses as writers and highlights the importance of self-correcting during the act of writing.

Students Have an Important Role in the Assessment of a Shared Lesson

Even though the teacher has provided the underlying structure of the lesson and endeavored to sustain the students' efforts and interest, students should play a role in the shared assessment following the composition of a text. They should consider the effort they expended in thinking along with the teacher, their contributions to the shared piece, their role as a group member, the level and nature of new understandings they acquired during the lesson, ways in which their previous understandings were amended or refined, and when and how they will use their learning. This assessment can sometimes be a "whole group" discussion, but on many occasions greater benefits will be achieved through partner or small-group sharing and of course, whenever possible, one-on-one discussion between teacher and student.

TWO EXAMPLES OF SHARED WRITING SESSIONS

The remainder of this chapter presents annotated excerpts from two shared writing sessions; the first from a fourth grade and the second from a seventh grade. They are offered as examples rather than recipes, for no lesson plan is totally transferable without some adaptation for the teacher's and the students' competencies and the desired learning outcome of the lesson. Only excerpts, including a selection of the students' responses, have been recorded here. The first lesson lasted fifteen minutes and the second twelve. Discussion with the teachers confirmed that these were the maximum lesson lengths for these students. The emphasis here is on explaining the teacher's role in the discussion, shown on a line by itself in italics. Student contributions or questions are in roman type. An ellipsis indicates the end of an excerpt from the lesson sequence. The work presented in the numbered figures is recorded in the sketch book used during reading and writing sessions. It is reviewed at the commencement of each lesson as a reminder of learning and its relevance to the week's learning target, and is revisited at the end of the lesson as a summary of new learning and further work needed toward achieving the desired outcome.

GLE 3.1.1[1] Narrows topic and elaborates using specific details
GLE 3.2.2 Uses language appropriate for specific audience and purpose
Activity: Expository texts, especially science

From the Grade 4 Teacher's Plan

While the children have some understandings about expository texts, the writing tends to be too general. I need to show how to keep the focus on a few points or questions. Attention to vocabulary will be key to revision and proofreading.

T: *Let's begin by reminding ourselves of our learning target for the week.* (Teacher reads from notes hand written on chart paper)

The Grade 4 Shared Writing Session

Learning Targets

We are learning to narrow our focus on a topic so we can include more detail.

We are learning to be more specific in our word choice—especially for both our purpose and our intended audience.

---

[1] *GLE refers to a curriculum requirement from a state document.*

T: *What does that mean? How will we know when we have achieved our target?*

S: We will not tell everything about a topic.

T: *Do we tell or explain and describe in an expository text?*

S: Explain and tell why or how or when.

S: And we won't lead our readers up the garden path.

T: *Can you tell us more about that?*

S: You only tell what you need to about one or two ideas or pieces of information.

S: And you give details.

S: Or examples.

T: *I think we will be able to add more success criteria or measures to let us know how far we are towards meeting our target after today's lesson. Who would like to walk us through our notes after we read the book about possums yesterday?*

S: First we listed what we already knew about expository texts and then we added what we had learned from the book.

Expository texts:

Main idea is clear to reader–it may be a theme or an issue	Reader needs to think what is not said and what they do/do not agree with
Explain rather than describe	Why and how are important
Details keep focus on topic and/or theme/issue	What is the author really saying?
Language is precise	Keep internalizing in own language
The conclusion is a summary	The summary keeps the reader thinking

T: *Can someone carry on explaining why we had added the two columns?*

S: The first column was what readers need to do when they read an expository book.

S: No, not what they have to do, but what they can do.

S: And you said that you would help us think about how that helps writers.

T: *Yes, that's what I would like us to think about today, but you could help me get started on my thinking as a writer. Can you think of anything from the list about reading that will help me?*

S: Don't you need a topic first?

T: *That's a good idea, because unless I have my topic or know why I am writing it, I cannot be sure that an expository text would be the best for it. I need to know quite a lot about my topic before I can write an expository text. So first I am thinking whether I am going to write about someone, something, or somewhere.*

S: It should be an animal because we are talking about animals that help the ecosystem.

T: *Well, I will choose wolves because I like wolves, I have read a lot about them, and there are some very interesting facts about their contribution to the environment and the ecosystem. I am thinking that most expository texts give specific information. I need to just narrow my writing to how wolves contribute to the ecosystem. I am not going to describe what a wolf looks like. I would like you to be my audience as well as my support group.*

. . .

I'll jot down some of my thoughts and then go back and number them in the order of importance. Number one will be my most important point, but that may not be what I write about first. It may be best to wait until the end when I use it as a summing up. (Teacher writes the following notes on a chart about her topic for writing)

1. Many have wrong idea about wolves
2. Do not attack humans
3. Live in packs-family groups
4. Run fast-strong legs, wide paws
5. Each has distinct howl-they howl, bark, snarl, whimper
6. Territorial
7. Efforts to save wolves

S: Why did you put strong legs in there? You said you were not going to describe them.

T: *Good point. But I might need to use that as a reason people think wolves are dangerous. Let's put a question mark there.* (Adds question mark to number 4) *This is how I think I am going to start my writing. I need to rehearse it again to make sure that it will capture your interest and that it tells you my topic and what I want you to know and think about wolves.*

. . .

I now need to get that written so I can see if it reads as well as it sounds. (Teacher adds the following writing to the chart)

The wolf is a much maligned creature with many people only thinking of wolves as the killers portrayed in fairy tales.

S: That tells a lot. Will all of your readers know what "maligned" means?

T: *That relates to one of our learning targets. Who is my audience?*

S: Us.

T: *Can you recall when we talked about the meaning?*

. . .

When I read my first paragraph, it seemed choppy. I need to try to get some good transitions between the sentences. Otherwise I don't think you will really read it thoughtfully. I think that gives a clearer picture.

. . .

One thing I know now is that I need to re-read each section or paragraph more than once. Perhaps you could help me here. As we read, let us check it makes sense for each of you. Perhaps some of you could read to check I have kept to the topic. I need to be thinking about the words and my spelling and the punctuation.

Knowing my first paragraph makes sense and lets my reader know where I am gives me confidence to think about the next paragraph. I need to think how I can make a slightly stronger case for my next point.

. . .

Let's now return to our chart about reading and writing expository texts and see what else we can add. What new learning have we achieved?

S: I thought you started with the best first but you put that last.

T: *That is similar to the story of "The Three Little Pigs." Think about the three houses and the order in which they were built.*

S: But in "Goldilocks and the Three Bears," the biggest one was last.

T: *Yes, but think where the main action was and the real point of the story.*

. . .

Thanks for helping me with this piece. I found the revision much easier because of your help.

S: It was easy when we looked for only one thing–not everything like we do.

T: *Yes, it is hard to try to fix everything in one read.*

At the end of the lesson, the teacher noted "GLE 1.3.1 Re-reads work several times and has a focus for each reading" in her work plan as a reminder of the focus for the next shared lesson.

The seventh-grade shared lesson was with a group of students identified by the teacher as being "straight-up writers whose writing lacked oomph." Several lessons had been devoted to revision with little apparent success, so she decided to focus on poetry, a genre listed in the state standards as a vehicle for using literary devices. Poetry was not a new form for the students– by seventh grade they had heard, read, and probably attempted writing po- ems and verse forms on many occasions. And a selection of poems had been read to the class in recent weeks.

An Example from Grade 7

T: *As I was driving to school one day last week I was blinded by the sun. Now that has happened before, but for some reason I keep think- ing about that particular morning. It is almost as if I need to keep that picture in my head because it was but a fleeting sight. All of a sudden– almost before I could fumble in my bag for my sunglasses–the brilliant light was gone. That has happened before, of course. But there was something special about the sun and the sky that morning. Sometimes we want to just remember or write about a fleeting moment. We don't want to write a whole story or even write a paragraph. I certainly don't want to write a long piece about the sun. Often a short poem or word picture is a good way to say a lot in a few words. I'll describe what I saw as best I can recall and then let's see if we can work together to record my experience in a brief piece. Question me as I try to describe it because I want you to try to build a picture in your head so you can help me when I try to write my piece. Perhaps one of you could jot down some ideas or words that might be useful when I write.*

My writing is certainly going to have to be more interesting than my telling or I will lose you! So I am thinking no extra words–tell it as if the camera stopped the world for a moment–use words that can make my readers (you folk) create a picture in their heads or make them think about a similar sight.

Where I saw it isn't important. What I saw is. What did I see? (Teacher writes the following on a chart)

An orange ball rolling across the sky

S: The sun doesn't roll. It glides.

S: No, when you glide you move fast. The sun doesn't go fast.

T: *You are absolutely correct. The sun was just there. The sky was blue and the sun a kind of vermillion color. I think suspended is a better word.* (Teacher writes on the chart again)

An orange ball suspended in the blue sea

T: *The sun was really in my face. It was almost as if it was saying "Here I am. Get up. Don't you know it is daytime?"* (The first six lines are composed and recorded with the students offering suggestions)

An orange ball suspended in the blue sea
Heralding a new day
Shrieking louder than the dawn chorus
As birds beckon the world to rise.
There it was bulging, big and bright
A statement of cheeriness and light.

T: *I have told enough about what I saw. It wasn't there for long, so I can't labor the description in my short piece of writing. I need to wake my readers up and let them know to switch their thinking or change the picture in their head.*

I have thought a lot about why, all of a sudden, the sky clouded over. It made me think about why people change. What makes us change from liking someone?

S: They do something nasty.

S: They change loyalty.

S: They are jealous.

T: *That's it.* (Teacher adds to the chart after "A statement of cheeriness and light")

> But alas—the clouds could not stand to see such glee
>
> So with jealous intensity

There was further discussion about the need to end a poem with a lingering thought, resulting in:

> An orange ball suspended in the blue sea
>
> Heralding a new day
>
> Shrieking louder than the dawn chorus
>
> As birds beckon the world to rise.
>
> There it was bulging, big and bright
>
> A statement of cheeriness and light.
>
> But alas—the clouds could not stand to see such glee
>
> So with jealous intensity
>
> Those puffs of white and gloomy grey
>
> Smoldered into a smoke screen
>
> Stealing us of our brief encounter
>
> Leaving us wondering
>
> What might have been.

T: *As I re-read this piece I am thinking about the three things I thought important to think about as I wrote. My readers were not with me when I saw the ball of fire. I needed to use precise language, but with enough detail to get a picture in your head. And I wanted my readers to keep thinking about something related to what they had read. You are my audience, so I am interested to hear what you think I have achieved. Read the piece to yourself and then talk among yourselves if you like.*

. . .

S: It's better than a long piece because it only says what it needs to.

S: Well, it makes you think because I don't know what might have been, like it says at the end.

S: You made the sun and the clouds act like people.

S: Yeah, that's what we learned is person–

S: Personification.

T: *I think poets use that device quite often. Perhaps you could think about that as you read some of the poems we have in our classroom. Did I give you enough information to make a picture in your head?*

S: You told us first but the short one is best. Even if we hadn't heard your first description, I would have got the picture.

T: *You know I am going to ask you to say why or how.*

S: Well, your word choice is better. It doesn't go on. You have to think as you read when things are left out for you to add.

. . .

T: *What does this make you think about your writing? Have you learned anything that will help you capture your readers' interest?*

S: I try to write too much and it gets boring.

S: I need to think about word choice.

T: *Both of those are good thoughts. I think word choice is a key to both. I find that rehearsing in my head what I want to say saves a lot of editing later. It is easier to get it right thinking it through than going back once it is written.*

The discussion continued about not being too quick to get something done and then not wanting to do any revision or correcting. The decision was made collectively that they would work for shorter pieces, attend to word choice, and make a commitment to revising their work. There was some discussion about revising each other's work, but the consensus among the students was that that could be a "cop out."

PART 2

Sharing the Magic

CHAPTER 3
Shared Reading
Brenda Parkes

Brenda Parkes is an international education consultant, children's author, and early literacy researcher. She has taught in New Zealand and Australia and spent twenty years as a teacher educator at Griffith University, Queensland. She has written several literacy programs and is the author of *Discovery Links,* an award-winning K-5 nonfiction guided reading program published by Newbridge Education.

For the past several years, Brenda has served as a literacy consultant for early childhood programs in Australia and the U.S. Most recently, she was a consultant for the shared reading component of a new content-area reading program—Reading PowerWorks™ (Sundance). She currently divides her time among consulting, writing, and speaking commitments. Her self-deprecating humor and her keen observations on the challenges that teachers face in today's classrooms keep her audiences engaged.

CHAPTER 4
Shared Writing
Jerry Miller

Jerry Miller is the Director of Instructional Support for the Issaquah School District in Washington State, where he oversees the Title II program for staff development and is responsible for K-12 reading, writing, and language programs for all students. He has served as a classroom teacher and a statewide reading specialist and is a nationally recognized speaker, staff developer, and author of many articles, book chapters, and materials for students. Jerry lives in Issaquah with his wife, Jan, who teaches second grade. Their daughters, Sarah and Anna, both live and work in Seattle. When they aren't working or writing, Jerry and his wife like to cook and entertain. Jerry's idea of the perfect weekend is to prepare and serve a home-cooked Chinese meal for twelve—or twenty . . .

	Desired Outcome	Student's Activity and Thinking	Support/Guidance	Teacher's Role	Approach
PART 1	Self-awareness	Observing Listening Absorbing *There is something in this for me. I want to be able to do likewise.*	Support	Modeling and inspiring Showing benefits of a skilled reader/writer in action	Read to or write for
PART 2	Self-correcting	Absorbing and practicing alongside a more knowledge-able other *I want to try to do this. I can practice with someone else.*	Support and guidance	Demonstrating–explicitly explaining–the "how" as well as the "what" to encourage participation	Shared reading/writing
PART 3	Self-assessing	Practicing and applying in other contexts *I can apply what I have learned as I practice by myself with someone watching and guiding me. I can overcome challenges by thinking about what I am learning. The more I practice, the easier it becomes.*	Guidance	Monitoring through interactive formative assessment (nurturing rather than measuring), questioning, provoking, focusing on how meaning is accessed	Guided reading/writing
PART 4	Self-improving	Gaining confidence in applying learning and meeting new challenges in self-selected contexts. *I can use what I have learned in other contexts. I can think about ways I can improve. I can use what I have learned to learn new things.*	Guidance and reflection	Observing, assessing through formal formative and perhaps some summative procedures, measuring effectiveness of learning and application Planning next learning target and learning opportunities	Independent reading/writing

Shared Reading
by Brenda Parkes

S hared reading involves a teacher and a student or group of students collaboratively thinking about, reading, and discussing particular aspects of a text. Based on the current interests, competencies, and needs of the learners, engaging texts are carefully chosen to support and extend their learning, ensure that they experience success, and help them see reading as worthwhile and relevant for their own interests and purposes.

This research-based instructional approach is a highly effective way to maximize student engagement and learning. It provides meaningful contexts for the teacher to explicitly demonstrate and scaffold students' understanding about how, what, and why writers write; how and why different kinds of texts are constructed; what language and text features typify different genres; how readers apply effective strategies to read different texts for different purposes; and how to use appropriate language to communicate insights, ideas, and perspectives about content.

As expert reader, the teacher takes the lead, explicitly demonstrating the nature and purpose of the text and the effective skills, strategies, and behaviors a fluent reader would use to capitalize on the supports and overcome the challenges to read and comprehend that text. These explicit demonstrations, in concert with carefully crafted explanations, questions, prompts, focused discussions, and invitations to join in the reading continuously engage and guide the students as thoughtful, active, successful participants.

Explicit teaching is intentional and direct. It focuses on demonstrating a technique that readers learn to control as a means to better comprehend (Pressley 2002). Students can all see and follow along with the clearly displayed text. They are encouraged and guided to play an active role throughout the lesson, listening and looking, thinking and responding, reading silently or orally with the teacher and classmates, and contributing to explicitly focused independent, partner, and whole group discussions. As each lesson unfolds,

---

the teacher observes how individuals participate. This information guides the amount and kind of explicit support provided and where responsibility for thinking, reading, and talking can be transferred to students, safe in the knowledge they will be successful while at the same time stretching their learning. Studies consistently show that this gradual release of responsibility (Pearson and Gallagher 1983) is a highly supportive and effective teaching practice.

Through successive experiences students gain in their confidence to think, read, and talk about texts and build control of a repertoire of effective strategies and the ability to apply them flexibly in different situations. Very importantly too, students experience success and with it the personal benefits and satisfaction reading is able to provide as they build confidence in themselves as learners.

THE CRITICAL ROLE OF LANGUAGE

Language development is a critical element of every shared reading experience. Within the flow of the lesson, the teacher ensures that students notice and think about how authors use words and grammar to communicate content and express perspectives and how the words and grammar support their comprehension of different kinds of texts. Explicit demonstrations and focused discussions model and provide practice with how to use oral language in different ways to communicate insights and perspectives and to consider and respond to alternate perspectives through dialogue with the teacher and members of the group.

The ability to understand and use language to:

  make associations between texts and experiences

  express personal thoughts and feelings

  raise questions and discuss content in appropriate ways and

  learn about language

is critical to comprehension. Shared reading provides opportunities to draw attention to ways language is used to structure and communicate the content of different texts and support students to use their own language and prior experience to share their questions about, and interpretations of, texts and experiences. Research studies (Gee 1994; Halliday and Hasan 1985; Wells 1999) show how language is used in different ways for different purposes, and how language learning is enhanced when it is used for real purposes, in authentic contexts. Shared reading provides both context and purpose.

Learning to talk about texts is enhanced by demonstrating reading as an ongoing conversation between an author and a reader and providing opportunities for students to engage in meaningful talk. When students understand that authors think about their intended audience and their purpose for writing before they make decisions about the way they will communicate their content and recognize different ways texts are communicated for different purposes, they will have a framework with which to question the author and text.

This talk strongly supports students' understanding and use of key vocabulary in content area texts. It is far more meaningful and enduring than teaching content words and their definitions prior to reading the text.

WHY USE SHARED READING IN GRADE 3 TO 8 CLASSROOMS?

Picture yourself with your new student group at the beginning of the school year. Many of them will have attended more than one school. All will have had more than one teacher and a range of literacy learning experiences that have shaped their perceptions of themselves as readers, writers, and learners. Some will enjoy reading and be able to flexibly apply effective strategies to comprehend a range of texts and text types. Others will read quickly and sound word perfect, but comprehend little. Still others will see school literacy as irrelevant to their needs and interests or simply unattainable and will have ways of avoiding engagement, or in Cris Tovani's words, "faking it" to get through the day.

Now consider the increasingly challenging and complex texts and text types these students will be required to read and understand, the purposes they will need to read for, and different ways they will be expected to communicate their insights, questions, and understandings. Science, social studies, and mathematics each bring new concepts, text structures, vocabulary, and ways of using language to communicate that are particular to that content area. In addition, they use increasingly sophisticated charts, tables, graphs, maps, and diagrams to impart, summarize, or synthesize information. Poems, biographies, plays, and novels pose their own challenges too, in content, organization, layout, language, and writing style.

SHARED READING MAXIMIZES AVAILABLE TIME AND SUPPORTS LEARNING

Although often perceived to be a K-2 approach, shared reading is a powerful instructional tool for making texts accessible and strategies for reading them transparent in all grade levels. As Regie Routman states, "Shared reading is an important missing piece in many reading programs, especially in grade 2 and above" (2003, 130). Shared reading not only allows you to explicitly teach how to access, comprehend, and communicate the information in different text types but to draw on the knowledge and experiences of all students in the group to build understanding about the content and effective reading strategies.

Integration of content area and literacy learning is time saving and meaningful, which is a huge bonus. The "hands on" experiences of science inquiry, social studies field trips and group projects, and mathematics manipulative materials and problem solving provide real-life experiences and accompanying language to connect with content area textbooks and shared reading texts. Active student involvement increases interest and engagement, enhances language and vocabulary development, provides opportunities for students to see themselves as successful readers, and bonds the group as they discover others who share their passions and interests, classmates who are experts on particular topics, and fellow researchers.

In summary, shared reading in the Grade 3 to 8 classroom will allow you to:

- Share the benefits and relevance of reading

- Integrate content and literacy teaching

- Explicitly model fluent reading and support students to engage in the thinking processes, strategies, and behaviors that a skilled reader uses

- Support students to gain and sustain meaning over longer texts

- Facilitate purposeful, inclusive discussion that enhances vocabulary development, understanding of concepts, and the ability to use language effectively across subject areas and topics to communicate insights, ideas, and questions

- Make text types, text structures, and text features accessible

- Show how multiple text features connect to contribute meaning

- Model how to set purposes and adjust reading rate

- Enable every student to participate and experience success.

WHAT DIFFERENTIATES K-2 SHARED READING FROM GRADES 3 TO 8?

Regardless of grade level, shared reading can draw students into the pleasures and personal rewards reading brings, demonstrate and progressively involve them in successful use of effective reading strategies, and enhance language facility. The major differences between shared reading in kindergarten to second-grade classrooms and shared reading beyond those grades lie in the competencies, needs, and interests of students; choice of materials and the purposes for which they are selected and used for explicit instruction; the length of time they are used; and the sophistication of discussion (see Figure 3.1).

ESTABLISHING ROLES, EXPECTATIONS, AND RHYTHMS

The ultimate goal of shared reading is to create a community of learners who enjoy reading, find reading personally useful, can flexibly apply effective strategies to read and comprehend different texts for different purposes, support each others' learning, and are able to think and talk about texts. This is first achieved by creating a physical setting that supports collaborative work. The best way to do this is to have students gather closely together on the floor. This enables them to all see, read, and learn from a text at the same time, easily form groups of two to three to carry out discussions, and compose short written responses. Once students are comfortable working this way, establish the roles and rhythms that

Kindergarten to Grade 2	Grades 3 to 8
Demonstrates the reading process and teaches students how to read	Demonstrates effective comprehension strategies for a wide range of text types
Mostly large group	Smaller needs-based groups for longer time, at point of need
Creates a store of familiar texts that are read and re-read for different purposes	Demonstrates how to read a variety of text types for different purposes
Builds knowledge about books and print	Builds knowledge about text features and genres
Lays the foundation for talking about texts	Extends talk about texts to include language used to communicate content-area concepts

Figure 3.1: How shared reading differs by grade level

build an expectation of purposeful learning, enjoyment, challenge, and success. Students must be actively involved at all times and know that their input will be heard, respected, and responded to.

Typically, the rhythm of a lesson includes a balance of introducing a text and engaging interest; drawing on relevant prior knowledge and experience to build background, setting purposes; demonstrating thinking and reading, inviting student thinking and talk, silent and oral reading; focusing student-to-student talk in groups of two or three, and sharing the group talk. Sometimes the teacher will read the whole piece and the students will follow along silently. This would be appropriate for a poetry selection that students could visualize as it was read to them, then read it themselves and contribute to a discussion about the particular parts of the text that evoked the images for them. However, maintaining momentum and engagement is critical. For that reason, never leave too long a gap without active student involvement or make explanations too long or involved. Students must know that they have an active role to play in what you are teaching.

The pattern of demonstration and interaction creates a web of shared meanings and experiences that can be drawn on and applied to other situations. It also creates bonds among students as they learn about each other as readers, writers, researchers, and individuals.

Although texts selected for shared reading in Grade 3 to 8 classrooms are mostly short, they are whole, continuous texts. This allows students to see how all aspects of the text work together to contribute meaning and provides a rich context for exploratory talk, particularly if the texts include real world examples that excite their interest.

CHOOSING INTERESTING, ACCESSIBLE TEXTS

Getting "buy in" to shared reading, particularly from disinterested or struggling readers, may be a challenge at first. Thankfully it is not an insurmountable one. The world is overflowing with suitable materials to use, including periodicals, newspaper articles and advertisements, poetry, plays, textbooks, songs, novels, instructions, picture books, and Internet text. Any of these can be presented on an overhead transparency as long as the print and visuals are large enough to be clearly seen. Posters, charts, and big books provide additional materials.

Start your collection of materials by surveying how the students use reading and writing for their own interests and purposes outside of school time. Find text feature correlations between the texts they want to read and the texts you need to teach. For example, sequence is a common text feature used in both science and social studies texts. Social studies texts typically show sequences as numbered steps or flowcharts, such as the one in Figure 3.2.

Instructions for downloading music onto an iPod or MP3 player, using a digital camera, operating a cell phone, or playing a computer game are also shown as sequences and would make a relevant, interesting introduction to this text feature. Not only will the material be of interest, but individual students can bring background knowledge and experience of the topic and contribute to or lead discussion. This will provide a frame of reference for science and social studies.

Suitable texts for shared reading should:

- Be of high interest, relevant, and informative

- Have an identifiable structure and purpose

- Mostly be able to be read in one session

- Support high-level thinking and discussion

- Enable **all** students to participate and be successful

- Connect reading to the real world and the curriculum.

Science and social studies texts frequently include cross-section diagrams such as that in Figure 3.3 to help students visualize information. Shared reading is an ideal way to introduce this text feature and to demonstrate how to read, think about, and talk about it before expecting students to understand it in concert with other print and pictures in that section of their science textbook.

Combining Hands-on Experience and Shared Reading to Demonstrate the Purpose of a Cross-Section Diagram

In this example, preceding the shared reading experience, students make and discuss cross-section models of a volcano. This provides concrete experience with the concept, language used to describe the concept, and language used to communicate understanding of and wonderings about the concept. The shared reading lesson links the student models to the cross-section diagram and shows how the diagram represents each part of the model. Later, when students read and discuss the relevant pages in their science textbook, they will be more able to comprehend the language, the concepts, and how the diagram integrates with the written text and photographs to provide information.

People in eastern Europe like to eat potato pancakes with sour cream or applesauce. You can enjoy them that way too!

How to Make Potato Pancakes

To serve four people, you need:

4 large potatoes
2 eggs
4 tablespoons of flour

1/2 teaspoon of baking powder
1/2 teaspoon of salt

1 First, peel the potatoes.

2 Next, grate the peeled potatoes.

3 Then, mix the grated potatoes with the eggs, flour, baking powder, and salt.

4 Last, fry spoonfuls of the potato mixture in oil until they are brown on both sides.

16

Figure 3.2: Flowchart in a social studies textbook
© 2004 by Newbridge Educational Publishing

VOLCANOES

Each volcano is different, but they all begin deep below **Earth's crust**, or outer layer, where huge blobs of melted rock called **magma** rise toward the surface. On the Ring of Fire, volcanoes form because, as the Pacific plate crashes or pushes under other plates, magma builds up. Filled with gases, hot magma can act a bit like a can of soda that is opened after being shaken. It can explode. When the magma **erupts**, or reaches the surface through a vent, it is called **lava**. Over time, layers of lava form a mountain around the vent. Both the mountain and the vent are called a volcano.

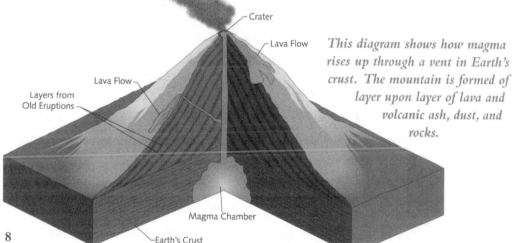

Crater

Lava Flow

This diagram shows how magma rises up through a vent in Earth's crust. The mountain is formed of layer upon layer of lava and volcanic ash, dust, and rocks.

Lava Flow

Layers from Old Eruptions

Magma Chamber

Earth's Crust

8

Figure 3.3: Diagram from a science textbook
© 2002 by Newbridge Educational Publishing

An Extract from a Fourth-Grade Shared Reading Lesson with a Fictional Picture Storybook

Purposes

◼ Share a fictional picture book based on history

◼ Demonstrate and guide discussion about how an author and illustrator build characterization

◼ Demonstrate and guide inferencing.

Preparation: Overhead transparencies of pages as shown.

Introduction

T: *This book,* The Memory Coat, *is written by Elvira Woodruff. She has written a number of fiction books based on history.* (Teacher shows cover picture) *In this book she tells the story of an immigrant family as they flee from war in Russia and their worry about not passing inspection at Ellis Island and being turned away. The story focuses on an orphaned boy, Grisha, who treasures and finds comfort in a coat his mother made him, and his friend Rachel, whose warm, noisy family have welcomed him into their lives. The illustrator, Michael Dooling, researched hundreds of photos to make sure his oil-painted illustrations show how the characters looked, dressed, and lived. At the end of the book, Elvira Woodruff details how she researched the topic.*

Setting a Purpose

T: *As I begin reading, I'd like you to listen and look and begin thinking about how the author and illustrator help you visualize the two main characters through their words and pictures. We are going to use that information to make inferences about the characters. To infer, you use your personal knowledge together with some clue or clues in the text to make a decision about something that is not explicitly written.*

What clues have the author and illustrator given to enable you to draw inferences from the front cover picture?

S: Rachel is most likely the one who decides things. She's already dressed ready to leave. It looks like she takes charge.

S: Maybe she's loaning him someone's coat. If it was his coat he could fasten his own buttons.

The teacher continues to show the pictures and written text and invite thinking as she reads about the noisy, happy family, the friendship between

Rachel and Grisha, and how Rachel would comfort Grisha when he grieved for his dead mother (Figure 3.4).

T: *What have you learned about Rachel so far?*

S: That she's like . . . kind.

T: *What makes you think that?*

S: It said she would go outside in the cold to comfort him.

S: On the front page she's helping him button up his coat . . .

At these times, Rachel's mother and grandmother worried about Grisha being outdoors in the cold, with only his threadbare coat to keep him warm. But whenever they offered to make him a new one, Grisha always refused.

"I like my coat the way it is," he would tell them sharply, and he'd race out into the icy wind.

Then Rachel would throw on her own warm, woolen coat and fly out the door to comfort him.

Figure 3.4: *The Memory Coat*
Text © 1999 by Elvira Woodruff; Illustrations © 1999 by Michael Dooling

---

CHAPTER 3 SHARED READING

T: *So you are noticing and connecting information in the language and illustrations. Has the author told you she was kind? Skim the text and check.*

S: No. She is telling about kind things Rachel does for Grisha.

S: How she helps him.

T: *So you are inferring from clues in the language that tell what she does, and clues in the illustrations that show what she does, which are both actions, together with your own thinking and experience about what being kind means. I like the way you are connecting the pieces of information. Let's write them in a two-column chart.*

Actions	Inference
Comforts Grisha	Is kind/helpful
Helps Grisha dress	

T: *What else did you notice or infer about the text and illustrations?*

S: She's not jealous.

T: *Where did you get that information?*

S: It says Grisha's come to live with her family and they're best friends.

T: *So you inferred from her actions that she could not be jealous if she had made friends with him. I like the way you thought that through. We'll add it to our chart.*

Let's focus on inferring about Grisha now. Reread the page silently, then turn to a partner and share your thinking about this question: Why do you think Grisha refused to have a new coat?

S: Maybe he thinks they'll throw away the old coat his mom made.

S: He likes it because it reminds him of her. It's his memory coat. He only wants to wear that coat.

S: He might think they'll laugh at him if he has a new coat and still wants to keep the old one.

T: *All your inferences make sense. I noticed another clue that supports your thinking as well. What does he say when he refuses?*

S: "I like my coat the way it is."

T: *And what does he do?*

S: He races outside.

S: I guess he does that so they won't know he's sad. Only Rachel knows.

T: *Help me add your inferences to our chart.* (Reading aloud as students silently read along or listen and look at the illustrations)

"War comes and the family is no longer safe to stay in Russia.

They sell what they own and buy tickets to journey to America."

T: *Read with me as much as you can. As you read, think how the information changes or confirms the way you visualize Grisha. Do they change or confirm your inferences?*

After reading the page, the students turn to a partner and discuss each focus before joining in a whole group response.

S: He's still too upset to talk about it in case they see him cry.

S: He relies on Rachel to defend him and explain.

T: *What are some reasons he might let her do the talking?*

Whole Group Shared Reading and Discussion from Figure 3.5 Text

"We must make a good impression, so that we'll all be allowed to stay in America," their grandfather told them, as the family gathered around the table for the last time. "If we make one mistake, we could be separated forever."

Everyone shuddered at the thought.

"There will be no mistakes," Rachel's father said.

"Then we'll have to do something about Grisha's coat," Bubba decided. "Look how torn and tattered it's become. If we're to make a good impression, he will have to have a new one. Come, Grisha, let me measure your arms."

"No!" Grisha cried. He grabbed the coat and ran to the attic to hide.

"*Tsk, tsk, tsk,*" his aunts and uncles clucked and shook their heads. "What can he see in such an old coat?"

"He sees the inside," Rachel whispered. "It's lined with the beautiful wool from his very own mother's coat. Inside, he can still feel his mama's touch."

"Ah." Their grandfather's sad sigh filled the room, as a fierce wind whistled around the windows. Everyone lowered their eyes, ashamed at having forgotten how Grisha's dear mother had struggled to make him the little coat in the last winter of her life. Not another word was spoken about it, and Bubba took out her basket to mend the coat once more.

Figure 3.5: Reading more of *The Memory Coat* during shared reading
Text © 1999 by Elvira Woodruff

S: She's part of the family and he's new. And he's quiet—he likes to draw what he's thinking. Rachel's the talker when they make up their stories.

S: He knows Rachel really understands what the coat means to him. When she says "he can still feel his mother's touch."

T (Adds the inferences to the chart): *Before we read the next pages, think of three words you would use to describe Rachel and three words to describe Grisha. Share them with a partner and how either the written text, illustrations, or an inference you have drawn from them has helped you make your decision. Use our chart to help you.*

Highlighter tape is used to identify the words and phrases for discussion. The words are listed, and the students discuss and decide which three the whole group feel best describe the characters so far.

Rachel-kind, strong, talkative

Grisha-quiet, timid, sad

T: *As you read this page with me, I want you to focus on Rachel. What has the author done here to help you understand her? What word could you add to her description now?*

(Paraphrased) *Grisha is turned back at Ellis Island because of a scratch on his eye. An X chalked on his coat to show he has been rejected. Quick thinking Rachel hides the X by turning the coat inside out, displaying the wool lining his mother had lovingly stitched for him. Another inspector realizes his sore eye is just a scratch and passes him and the family to begin their new life in America.*

S: The author has shown Rachel can think quickly.

S: She's quick witted.

S: Resourceful, too.

T. *Tell us more about why you describe her as resourceful.*

S: She solved several things at once. She remembered his mother had sewn the woolen lining in the coat. She knew the chalk mark wouldn't show on the inside. And she took him to a different inspector from the first one that had turned him away.

S: She's brave, too. She wasn't too scared to try to help him.

T: *Has anyone noticed another big inference we could draw? Think about the coat.*

USING BIG BOOKS

Many big books that include the concepts, content, text, and language features of science, mathematics, social studies, literature, plays, and poems are published for shared reading in Grade 3 to 8 classrooms. Quality nonfiction choices for older readers can be found in Read to Learn: Social Studies and the Ranger Rick Science Program (both from Newbridge). These engaging big books cover a wide range of standards-based content and support the research skills of students. *The Wolf's Story* (Parkes 2001), written as rap, is ideal for building fluency. It is designed to support re-reading, dramatization, debate, and writing as readers consider the traditional tale from the perspective of the wolf and a shady cast of friends. The key to choosing these resources is their potential to interest and engage your students; how closely they fit with state standards and curriculum content; how clearly they communicate and invite dialogue about the information; and to what extent they can be used for different purposes at different times.

The title of the science big book shown in Figure 3.6, *Exploring Everyday Wonders* (Lunis and White 2000), promises active involvement and relevance.

Figure 3.6: A big book on science
© 2000 by Newbridge Educational Publishing

The double-page spread supports the science processes of observing, explaining, hypothesizing, asking questions, interpreting data, and drawing conclusions to unlock the science secret in this everyday wonder. The two pages are rich with opportunities for purposeful reading, thinking, talking, and learning. To read and comprehend the content, the teacher demonstrates how readers draw on existing knowledge and experience, make and check predictions, use the scaffold provided by the consistent layout and text structure on each double-page spread, monitor meaning, adjust reading pace, synthesize, infer, and re-read by drawing on and integrating information in photographs and text.

Each double-page spread provides a different example of an everyday wonder for students to interpret by applying the processes of scientific inquiry in concert with effective reading strategies and dialogue. Hands-on experience before, during, and after the reading scaffold students to use the language of science and learn the concepts as they read, write, talk, and inquire. The layout and headings remain the same, providing a predictable structure and the opportunity for more than one lesson for those students who would benefit from a second experience. The book is also an ideal resource for follow-up paired, small-group, and independent work for others as well as a model for student writing.

AN EXTRACT FROM A GRADE 4 SHARED READING LESSON USING A BIG BOOK ON SCIENCE

In this lesson, Gloria, a teacher of fourth-grade students, is using the 5 E's Model–Engagement, Exploration, Explanation, Elaboration, and Evaluation–to explore the concept of condensation. She initiates **Engagement** by guiding students to observe the photo on page 4 of a big book that describes and illustrates everyday wonders.

> T: *What do you see?*
>
> S: Water on the grass.
>
> S: Drops of water on the grass.
>
> T: *What do you think happened? What could you infer?*
>
> S: It could have been raining.
>
> S: Someone could have been watering the lawn.
>
> T: *That's good thinking. Could it have been anything else?*
>
> S: Maybe someone spilled a container of water.
>
> S: Someone wasted water.

T: *Listen and think as I read the text.* (Reads text shown on left-hand page in Figure 3.6) *Would the time of day affect your thinking? Have you ever walked in the grass early in the morning and got your feet wet?*

S: (Several answer) Yes.

T: *What made the grass wet?*

S: A rain shower.

Gloria prompts the group to think about the photo and caption at the bottom of page 5.

T: *Look at the photo beside the yellow caption. What do you observe?*

S: Ice cubes in the water.

S: Drops of water on the outside of the glass.

T: *What caused the drops of water? Read with me.* (They read the caption together) *Now go back to our first observation on page 4. How has your thinking changed?*

S: I don't think the water came from rain or someone watering.

T: *If I said to you it was condensation, what kind of definition would you give condensation?*

S: If it's hot air inside our classroom and cold air outside the water might collect on the inside window pane.

T: *So condensation might be caused by temperature? We're going to make some observations to learn more about condensation.*

Groups of students are given a glass of water with ice cubes in it and two thermometers. One thermometer is placed inside the glass and one outside. Students record the temperature outside the glass, then take the temperature every minute on the thermometer inside the glass to observe at what point the drops begin to form on the outside of the glass. Students chart the data, which is used to construct a line graph showing the dew point.

Exploration

T: *Now read the science secret on page 5 with me. What can you infer from that about the dew?*

Explanation

S: The night must have been cooler than the morning.

S: The temperature must have dropped during the night.

T: *How can you infer that?*

S: The drops collected on the glass as the temperature dropped.

CHAPTER 3 SHARED READING

S: And cool air changed the water vapor in the air.

S: It changed it from a gas to a liquid.

S: It caused the moisture to come out of the air.

T: *So how would you define condensation?*

S: Condensation is where water vapor changes from a gas to a liquid.

T: *And what causes condensation?*

S: The change in temperature. The air has to be cool enough for moisture to form.

By integrating the shared reading experience into the 5 E's model, students have had the opportunity to encounter and use the new words and concepts, together with the language of science that guides inquiry and discussion, in a variety of contexts. In this way they begin to make the language and concepts their own—to be drawn on in future learning experiences. Gordon Wells' (1999) research on situated language supports language learning in real contexts, as does J. P. Gee, who states, "reading and writing are fully embedded in and integrated with learning, using and talking about specific content" (Saul 2004).

Used appropriately to support students' needs and to engage their interest, shared reading has much to offer in Grade 3 to 8 classrooms. It can build on read-aloud experiences with fiction and nonfiction and lay the foundation for students to apply the demonstrated skills, strategies, and behaviors with increasing independence in guided and independent reading. Most importantly, it can help students to read with understanding, view themselves as successful readers and learners, discuss their reading and learning, pose questions, engage in inquiry, and enjoy reading. For these reasons it more than earns a place in your third- to eighth-grade classroom.

Shared Writing
by Jerry Miller

CHAPTER

4

I am a firm adherent to the workshop model of writing instruction, in which I have, for decades, seen the power of making a safe environment where time, choice, and responsibility are given to readers and writers along with modeling, instruction, direction, and an ever-increasing expectation for evolving skill and strategy development.

I have borne witness to dazzling pieces of fiction and memoirs in elementary classrooms, wherein students self-selected topics and publishing formats; where they followed a writing process model to work their way through constructing or reconstructing whole worlds on the page. And, in those same classrooms, I have watched and waited in vain for some students to catch the spark and produce something in which they could take justified pride of authorship. When, while watching and waiting, should I have intervened?

> How do I teach students about different forms of writing without stunting them with prescribed formats and stifling formulas?

> How do I point out the underlying logic in various content areas without stunting curiosity and discovery?

> Am I remaining faithful to process writing if I prescribe writing tasks to determine student skill level?

> Must prompted writing be necessarily joyless? Must students select all their own topics? When do I intervene and where? In topic choice? Form and format?

As teacher and student negotiate their way through a shared writing session, questions such as these form the heart of explicit writing instruction in the intermediate grades.

"Knowing" and "knowing about" are two different things. Many of my early writing lessons were about exposing students to one aspect of writing or another, but the exposure didn't go deep enough. In an effort to provide student choice and to keep myself from stifling creativity, I hoped that they would come to knowledge through exposure alone. I have come to see the value in explaining and demonstrating a specific skill–talking through the reasons for employing it, the logic behind it, and the art of knowing when to employ it. Next, I focus on using the skill in a shared or guided writing or revision session, and finally, I think about setting both the environment and the expectation that will result in my students employing the skill independently. Crucial to this sequence is knowing how much front loading to do, and how much time to spend on a particular set of skills or strategies so that students deeply understand them. For some students, modeling alone is sufficient, but for others, multiple demonstrations, discussions, and exposures to the work of other, more sophisticated, authors are called for. A few others may need even more scaffolding and support.

Matching students to the appropriate amount of direction can only happen after several things are firmly in place. First, the teacher must know, absolutely, what constitutes excellent writing for students at the grade level he or she is teaching. Second, the teacher must have an intimate knowledge of what each student in the class is capable of doing independently and of what each can do with support. Frequent and continual conversation between teacher and student at each stage of the writing process is essential, as is ongoing observation of students as they work. Examination and monitoring of student self-assessment is key as well.

Deciding "how much" to share with writers is one issue. Deciding the logistics of that sharing is another. One of the impediments that a teacher encounters when writing with older students is the fact that their pieces tend to be lengthy. Writing out a multi-chapter narrative or a report with several subtopics is a burdensome process when using chart paper and markers and tape. Technology has come to the rescue in this case, in the form of document projectors and LCD machines that allow a teacher to write with students quickly and efficiently. A moderate facility with a word processing program and the highlighting, editing, and drawing toolbars allows teachers and students to try their ideas on the spot.

Because digital texts can be copied and saved, the same piece can be used any number of times to demonstrate and practice writing skills without taking valuable group time to produce new text. This practice underscores a concept we attempt to teach in reading: namely, that we return to texts over and over again for different purposes throughout our lives.

During shared reading, the teacher "lifts the veil" and allows students to experience the thought processes that take place as a competent "maker of meaning" goes about his or her work. This process makes conscious the unconscious interplay of reader, text, and context that takes place in a reader's mind. As teachers, we share this inner dialogue with our students so that they can be made aware of and control their own thought processes as they read. In shared reading, we are making the invisible visible–the unconscious conscious–for, though we hold books in our hands, feel their weight and substance, though we turn pages or, in the current era, click on new windows and screens, the real work of reading takes place in the head, unseen.

Unlike reading, we can trace the evolution of our own thinking about writing as we draft and revise onto paper. Much of the work of writing, though, still takes place cerebrally. It is this inner dialogue that teachers want to highlight and focus upon during shared writing.

First, we identify which questions must be addressed as we prepare to write.

> What am I going to write about?
>
> How am I going to keep the topic manageable?
>
> For whom am I writing?
>
> What do I know about my audience?
>
> Why am I writing this? What effect do I hope to achieve?
>
> What specific format will this writing take?

Next, we articulate our decision-making as we draft. While we isolate, weigh, and give shape to our ideas on paper, we constantly shift from the perspective of writer to reader and back again.

> How will I introduce my topic or my characters?
>
> How will I organize this piece?
>
> What is most important here?
>
> How will I develop my characters?
>
> What images am I creating?
>
> What am I assuming the audience already knows?
>
> Is this making sense?

CHAPTER **4** SHARED WRITING

During revision we ask yet another set of questions:

Was this what I really meant to say?

Are my readers going to get my message?

Could I have said things more clearly or more accurately?

Have I included enough details? Have I included the right details?

Which of these sentences is unnecessary?

Does it sound right?

GETTING STARTED

In order to implement shared writing effectively, teachers must have a very clear idea of what, exactly, they want their students to know and be able to produce through the writing process. Every exchange between teacher and students should help to make that expectation clearer and more easily attainable. The first step in getting started, then, is to review your district or state standards for student writing. What does exemplary writing look and sound like at the grade level you teach? Which forms are expected of your students, and at what level of complexity?

Once you know the target skills you are trying to foster, start collecting exemplars of each specific aspect of writing on which you intend to focus. Students should be surrounded by examples, both professionally written and student generated, that show them, explicitly, what is expected in any format they will be asked to master.

Developing, adding to, and using classroom-generated rubrics are also essential aspects of effective shared writing. Rubrics should reflect the evolving sophistication of young writers by being updated throughout the year as students' skills mature. When teachers create rubrics on their own, or only share them with students after the fact as an evaluation tool, their power as an instructional tool is lost. Well-written rubrics should lead students, naturally, to revision.

All the preparation and planning and rubric building in the world will not lead to effective shared writing instruction, though, if we don't know the abilities and interests of our students. We get to know our writers through conferencing with individuals about their stories, reading works in progress as well as finished pieces, and attending closely to what students elect to share during author's chair. Knowing what our students know permits us to move quickly into that realm where teacher support and student independence allow learning to take place.

WHOLE GROUP VERSUS SMALL GROUP SHARED WRITING

Shared writing is suitable for either whole group or small group instruction. The specific setting does determine, though, the degree of depth that can be covered during the lesson. In a whole group setting, the content of shared writing lessons tends to be more general and over-arching. This stands to reason, as an entire class represents a broad range of interests, skill levels, and readiness. Some students will be thinking about the topic under discussion for the first time, while for others participating in the discussion will serve as review and refinement of understanding. Small groups, brought together around a common writing task, project, or problem, can focus in greater depth and specificity on a particular component of writing. Because skill levels tend to be more similar in small groups, shared writing can be more rigorous and more specific.

Shared writing sessions with a whole group might focus on any of the following:

Identifying the writing task through an examination of:

■ Topic Choice

■ Audience

■ Purpose

■ Writing forms and features.

Exploring and revising for the six traits of quality writing:

■ Ideas

■ Organization

■ Word Choice

■ Sentence Fluency

■ Voice

■ Conventions.

Reviewing and refining individual stages of the writing process.

Small group shared writing can focus on the intersection of task and trait and process. For example, how does my audience affect the ideas I share or the vocabulary I use to convey them? How does my purpose shape the organizational structure of my finished product? The chart in Figure 4.1 outlines some questions that teachers might use to begin this type of shared exploration. These questions give our students a sense of the sort of ongoing inner dialogue that writers employ. They can also serve as potential areas of focus for shared writing lessons and more explicit instruction.

SHARED WRITING IN ACTION: A DEMONSTRATION LESSON

I'd been invited into Carolyn Lesh's classroom to give a shared writing lesson. Carolyn and I had spoken in depth about the abilities of her students. This was a group of very high-performing fourth graders. They enjoyed writing and had a fairly sophisticated set of skills in place already. An ongoing challenge for these students had been writing from perspectives other than their own. The focus of our time together would be "Ghost Writing"–telling someone else's story as if it is your own. My goal was to target the depth and breadth of questions the writer must ask if he or she is going to write a story from someone else's perspective.

As I entered the classroom, Carolyn had her students in groups of four, sitting around common tables. Each student had a writing journal and several pencils at the ready. I had a chart stand with lined paper and markers set up in the front of the room and a laptop computer and LCD projector focused toward a screen next to the chart stand. On the chart I had already written the words Who, What, Where, When, and Why, under the heading, Recount. We had chosen recount for this writing experience because it would force us to "live in another's skin" as we wrote from the perspective of someone else. I wanted to move the students through review and directly into new learning as quickly as possible. After a brief introduction and conversation about writing in general, I launched into the day's topic:

"Often someone has an intriguing story to tell, or they have done something that would make an excellent story, but they are not accomplished writers. These people tell their story to someone who is a writer, and then the writer constructs the story as if it were about himself. The person who writes the story is called the 'ghost writer' because he or she remains hidden, while the person about whom the story is written is given total or partial credit for the writing.

	Topic	Audience	Purpose	Form
Ideas	What do we know about this topic? What do I need to research? Where will we find the information we need? Which facts do I need to double check?	What will be interesting to the audience? What does my audience already know? How much background information must I provide? How will I make my intent clear?	Which facts are crucial and which are supportive? Which facts need supporting information and details in order to be made clear? How will my use of details lead the reader to the conclusion or effect I want?	Does the subject matter I have chosen lend itself to the form of writing that is expected?
Organization	What is the logical framework underpinning the content area of the topic I've selected? Cause/Effect Question/Answer Sequential Order Compare/Contrast	What does my audience expect from this form of writing? What do they already know about the form? How will I let them know the form of writing I am attempting?	What will this piece of writing lead readers to do, think, or feel? Will it contribute to their understanding, affirm or challenge their beliefs, or prompt them to take action of some kind?	What is the expected physical layout (format) for this form? What are the component parts of this form?
Word Choice	What specialized language surrounds this topic? Which specific vocabulary do I need to be clearer on?	What is the expected register of language used by this audience? Which vocabulary will they already know and which must I define?	Will I be employing the language of story, of questioning and inquiry, of cause and effect, of description, and so on?	Which transitions are the hallmarks of this form of thinking?
Sentence Fluency	Are my sentences a match with the complexity of the ideas I am trying to convey? Does the rhythm and cadence of my sentence carry the reader from thought to thought?	Am I writing in a style that is recognizable to and appropriate for my audience?	What mood am I trying to create? How will my sentences give the feeling of confident authority, excite, frighten, calm, or surprise?	What punctuation is expected in the types of sentences I am using?

Figure 4.1: Questions to guide a writer's inner dialogue

© 2006 by Richard C. Owen Publishers, Inc.

(Figure continued)

	Topic	Audience	Purpose	Form
Voice	Have I chosen a voice that matches my subject matter and the purpose for my writing?	Is the voice I have chosen appropriate for my audience? Will my approach and language be familiar and inviting to my readers?	Do my style and approach and the mood I am trying to create achieve the desired effect?	Is the voice I have chosen the one usually associated with this type of writing?
Conventions	What are the specialized symbols or words that are unique to this topic or field of study?	How will I employ the conventions of the English language to precisely and deliberately communicate with my audience? What do they expect to encounter as they work through my text?	How will I apply and appropriately "bend" the rules of grammar and punctuation in order to create the desired effect?	What is the expected structure for this form? What physical layout makes the most sense for my purpose?

Figure 4.1: *(Continued from previous page)*

"If you look at the autobiographies and biographies of sports players, you will often see the phrase, 'As told by _____.' This is one way publishers let readers know that a ghost writer was involved in crafting the book.

"Today we are going to take a crack at being ghost writers for your teacher, Mrs. Lesh. I have asked her to think of something memorable that happened when she was a little girl. We'll listen to her story and then re-write it as if we were Mrs. Lesh. Before we have her tell her story, though, let's remind her of the basic things a recount must include." Pointing to the chart at the front of the room, I reminded Mrs. Lesh (and the rest of the class) about the basic format and purpose of a recount. *"What other questions do we want Mrs. Lesh to be sure to answer so that we will be able to re-write her story?"*

At this point, students generated a list of things they wanted Mrs. Lesh to be certain to include. As they asked questions, I added them to the chart in front of the room, leaving space for abbreviated notes if needed:

How old were you?

Where did you live?

What did you wear?

What kind of a little girl were you?

Who all was in the story?

What happened when (in what order)?

Is this a true story?

As the teacher prepared to tell her story, students opened their writing journals and got ready to take notes.

Mrs. Lesh then told a story about staying with her very formal and quiet, and, as it turns out, slightly unnerving "Aunt Sister," in the town of Texarkana, Texas when she was five years old. In an effort to liven things up, she hid behind a door and jumped out to frighten her aunt. Aunt Sister was, indeed, frightened, but she was also mortified at her young niece's outburst. "Don't ever scream like that again, or the neighbors will phone the police," she scolded.

Later, aunt and niece lay down together for afternoon naps. Just as they were going off to sleep, they saw a police car making its way up the street. "See," Aunt Sister whispered, "There are the police looking for that loud little girl right now."

After giving students a few minutes to finish their note taking, I asked, *"Are there other questions you wish we had asked your teacher before she began telling the story?"* As students blurted out their additional questions, I added to the list on the chart in front of the room:

What did your parents do?

Why were you at your aunt's house?

Were the police really looking for you?

What did your aunt's house look like?

What kind of furniture did she have?

What did she look like, and what did she wear?

Why was she so quiet?

What was the neighborhood like around your aunt's house?

What were the curtains like on the window in the room where you were napping?

Were you scared of your aunt after that? Did you ever go back again? Was she serious, or was she just trying to scare you?

What were you called when you were five years old?

After the students generated their questions, Mrs. Lesh kindly "filled in the missing pieces" of her recount. The students and I jotted notes—I on the chart paper, and they in their notebooks.

"Now it's time to ghost write. Remember, we have to approach this as if we were Mrs. Lesh. What words will we use to give the impression that we are an adult recalling something that happened when we were younger? Someone start us out, and I'll take dictation."

Lynn, who had already begun sketching out a paragraph on another piece of journal paper, raised her hand and offered the first attempt, which I entered into the laptop and projected in front of the whole group:

Before she was Mrs. Lesh, she was Carolyn.

"That's a start," I said. *"Our audience for this piece thinks this is actually being written by Mrs. Lesh. Does our first sentence give that impression?"* A discussion followed about needing to write in first person and using the appropriate pronouns. Another student pointed out that Mrs. Lesh had shared the nickname her family had for her when she was five. After two or three tries, our lead had evolved nicely:

Before I was Mrs. Lesh, I was called Carolyn, but before my friends called me Carolyn, my family called me "Little Sue-Sue."

"Now, how are we going to let the readers know about Sue-Sue's character? Remember your teacher said she was a 'proper little southern girl, but she liked to race around with her brother'."

Rich popped in, "Why don't we just say she—no, **I** was a tomboy?"

"We could do that, but is there a way we could let the audience figure out she was a tomboy without saying it up front? Did we get any information from your teacher we could put together to show, rather than tell about, her personality?"

"Give it a three-minute try in your journals and we'll see what happens." During shared writing experiences with older students, I frequently ask them to take three or four minutes to respond to a question or to attempt to solve a problem on their own before we discuss it as a whole group. This allows all the students time to think and respond. I find this strategy especially helpful if there are two or three excited contributors in the class whose comments begin to eclipse those of less confident writers. When the writing time was up, several students suggested sentences that described young Sue-Sue. Through discussion and trial and error, we finally agreed to the following:

> Before I was Mrs. Lesh, I was called Carolyn, and before my friends called me Carolyn, my family called me "Little Sue-Sue." Five-year-old girls acted differently then than now. For one thing, I never wore pants–even to play in the dirt or to climb trees or to race my brother down the long dirt driveway to the mailbox. My mother always dressed me in proper little sun dresses, then braided my long, straight, brown hair and tied the ends with ribbons that jumped and bounced as I ran through my father's watermelon fields.

I asked the students to remember that the majority of the action in this story took place at Sue-Sue's aunt's house in town. *"How are we going to get Sue-Sue to town and into her aunt's house so that the action can begin?"* This time, before writing in their journals, students brainstormed in their four-person table groups how best to proceed. As students spoke, I copied snippets of their conversation onto the screen for us to consider:

Her aunt always took care of her when her family went to town.

She never had a babysitter.

The aunt was called Sister because she was Sue-Sue's father's sister.

Her aunt lived on a street with sidewalks and green grass and oak trees.

Her aunt's house was perfect.

Her aunt was always perfect.

Her aunt liked everything quiet and peaceful.

Her aunt was a perfectionist.

Her aunt was a proper lady.

It quickly became apparent that the students were far more focused on the aunt and how different she was from Sue-Sue than the mechanics of getting the niece to the aunt's house. Rather than spending a great deal of time on getting the characters from place to place, I decided to move them along to character description. The main reason for this change was practicality; our time together was brief. Were I the regular classroom teacher, or if I had been scheduled to work with this group of students over the course of several days, I might have brought them back to moving characters from place to place. Instead, I "filled in" and we pushed on.

"I'm going to write a transition sentence to get the action started. Then, I want us to look at the list of statements I overheard while you were talking and see if we can describe Aunt Sister by comparing and contrasting her with Sue-Sue."

Whenever my parents had business in town, I was dropped off to stay with my aunt, who everybody called "Sister." Going to her house was like going to another world.

"Now, what were the major differences we can write about?"

Their neighborhoods were different

Their houses were different

Their clothes were different

Sue-Sue's family was fun, but Aunt Sister was serious. She had rules for everything.

Each group of students began to craft a set of sentences contrasting whatever element they'd chosen. As they worked, I moved from group to group, gently nudging them to combine ideas and polish sentences and encouraging them to ask their teacher for missing details. Mrs. Lesh not only answered their questions but also added them to the list we had been making at the front of the room. Because I was aware of what the other groups had written, I made suggestions that would help the individual paragraphs flow into a coherent narrative when we combined the writing from the various groups into our single recount.

Another fifteen minutes passed and we had added considerably to our recount:

> Our dirt driveway was lined, on either side, with watermelon vines that baked in the hot Texas sunshine. Both sides of Sister's paved street were covered over by the long branches of oak trees that reached out and touched one another high above the street, making shade, even on the hottest day. By the time we got to Sister's door, the ribbons in my braids were usually coming undone, and I'd managed to get dust on my sun dress. After ringing her doorbell, I always brushed the dust off my dress and ankles, and stood as tall and straight and still as I could.
>
> When she came to the door, Aunt Sister wore a perfectly ironed dress, with every button fastened "just so." Each hair on her head was combed into place and seemed to stay where it was, no matter what she was doing. Sister never ran, never hurried, never even spoke quickly. Everything about her was slow and calm and perfect.

At this point, my scheduled visit was coming to an end. I had purposefully led us to the point where the defining action in the story was about to take place. Now, as students had an appreciation for the amount of detail and specificity they needed to add to the story, they were free to write the remainder on their own. I left them a printed draft of our story to this point, and the chart—which had gone to four pages—filled with questions.

A week later I received a set of delightful retells of their teacher's childhood memory, along with a note from Mrs. Lesh. She followed this experience with another project in which students worked in pairs to each retell a memory for his or her partner to ghost write. During the second experience, their teacher noted that students' questioning was much more thorough and detailed and the notion of perspective was clearly assimilated into their writing.

Note that, although this lesson was primarily about asking questions, many other aspects of writing were touched upon: word choice, point of view, character development, inferring about audience, developing a story line, using transitions, and elaboration through comparison and contrast. When teachers employ shared writing strategies, they must be prepared to go where the students' questions lead, and then to gently bring them back to the task at hand. This can feel daunting if the teacher is not clear about the desired outcome or focus of the lesson.

The shared writing lesson above focuses on a new piece. More frequently in the intermediate grades, I develop shared writing lessons around a previously written draft. Perhaps a more appropriate title, given the percentage of time this strategy is employed, would be "shared revision." Pointing out new strategies, reinforcing developing skills, and sharing the thinking and decision-making that takes place as a writer practices his or her craft is much easier once there is text on the page. Beginning with a "revisable" text focuses the discussion on the skill or strategy I want to highlight without having to take the time to develop text with which to work. Introducing sentence combining for fluency, adding details to help clarify and strengthen ideas, and editing for word choice are three areas where I always begin with a pre-written text.

SOME THOUGHTS ON FORMULAIC WRITING

As students progress through the elementary grades, the tension between a focus on product and a focus on process intensifies. Curricular demands increase exponentially as content area subjects are introduced and elaborated. Further exacerbating the pressure to produce, large-scale, high-stakes assessments are introduced by third or fourth grade, and mounting public cries for accountability fuel the perception that we must get our students to deliver concise, accurate, acceptable responses to decontextualized writing prompts.

An increasingly popular response to this "pressure to produce" is the use of writing frames and formulas. Although initially developed for the most struggling students, these are being given to all students in many schools as **the** method for composing a sentence, a paragraph, an essay, or literary criticism. But having students produce something that looks like writing is not the same as producing students who can write. Providing a frame or formula to a struggling writer, or assisting a group in reading a couple of well written pieces and deriving a formula which they, then, emulate, is one support we can provide. It does provide a skeleton onto which the student can build a body. But, that support quickly becomes a confinement if teachers do not ease students back off the formula once the underlying structure and logic is understood. For, while struggling students may learn to follow a formula exactly, unless they also learn to function outside that formula, their works never come to life.

There are a number of pitfalls in the use of formulaic writing. First, those who truly struggle see each part of the formula as a separate entity. The five sentence paragraph, for example, is painstakingly constructed of five separate sentences. One introduces, three expand, the final summarizes. But they frequently don't hang together because the student doesn't have an overarching concept of what he is trying to say. Instead, he is obsessed with filling in the five lines. There are no transitions, and the piece does not deliver a coherent message. This student wants a greater understanding of the logic that underlies a paragraph, and a clearer understanding of the needs of his audience. He needs many experiences with many types of paragraphs and many discussions with teachers and peers about what, exactly, all paragraphs have in common: one central theme, point, or message, expanded upon with details, examples, or explanations, and linked logically with that which preceded it and that which follows.

Share formulas for writing judiciously. I limit their use to individual students who have not tasted success in writing prior to coming to my classroom and who are not readily participating in and learning from shared writing experiences. These students, by Grade 3, are usually thoroughly discouraged and believe they simply cannot write. Sometimes, giving them a formula allows them to gain a few "writing miles," and in so doing, allows them a sense of what completing a paragraph "feels like." Do not force already competent writers to use a tool developed for those who struggle. If you are planning to teach formulaic writing, have a plan, prior to introducing frames, for how you are going to wean students off the formula and into independence. Remember that they are only a means to an end, and not, in and of themselves, sufficient to pass as writing.

Finally, as Margaret noted in the introduction, the trend in the intermediate grades is to shorten the formal writing block in order to accommodate expanded content in other subject areas. I would like to suggest that writing becomes the underlying focus of the entire day once students reach third grade. By this I mean that writing, and reading, are the vehicles that carry the content. Teachers often bemoan the lack of "authentic" opportunities for students to write when the very opportunities they are seeking are embedded in the rest of their teaching day. Shared writing doesn't have to happen just at writer's workshop time. A shared writing lesson on clear and concise procedures is appropriate both during a science lesson and as a follow-up to an art lesson. Studying content by actively and explicitly studying how authors write **about** content provides the underlying logical and organizational framework that allows students to carry learning from one discipline to another.

PART 3

Keeping the Magic Alive

CHAPTER 5

Guiding Readers to Independence
Erin Lucich

Erin Lucich has taught students in kindergarten through fifth grade as a classroom teacher and a reading specialist. She has worked as a literacy coach and teacher developer and, most recently, as a trainer of coaches for her school district in Vancouver, Washington. Erin is an avid learner and in that way views her writing as a temporary record of thought, destined to be revised and re-written many times over. Erin lives with her family in the Northwest.

CHAPTER 6

Guiding Writers to Independence
Margaret E. Mooney

Margaret Mooney is a teacher, writer, and consultant dividing her time between her homeland of New Zealand and the United States. Much of her current work focuses on the interdependence of reading and writing, where one of her mantras is "You learned from an author-now use 'it' as an author." When she is not teaching or writing, her moments are filled with writing (yes, for pleasure), quilting (her latest obsession), and gardening (her obsession until quilting came along).

	Desired Outcome	Student's Activity and Thinking	Support/Guidance	Teacher's Role	Approach
PART 1	Self-awareness	Observing Listening Absorbing *There is something in this for me. I want to be able to do likewise.*	Support	Modeling and inspiring Showing benefits of a skilled reader/ writer in action	Read to or write for
PART 2	Self-correcting	Absorbing and practicing alongside a more knowledge-able other *I want to try to do this. I can practice with someone else.*	Support and guidance	Demonstrating– explicitly explaining– the "how" as well as the "what" to encour-age participation	Shared reading/ writing
PART 3	Self-assessing	Practicing and applying in other contexts *I can apply what I have learned as I practice by myself with someone watching and guid-ing me. I can over-come challenges by thinking about what I am learning. The more I practice, the easier it becomes.*	Guidance	Monitoring through interactive forma-tive assessment (nurturing rather than measuring), questioning, provok-ing, focusing on how meaning is accessed	Guided reading/ writing
PART 4	Self-improving	Gaining confidence in applying learning and meeting new challenges in self-selected contexts. *I can use what I have learned in other contexts. I can think about ways I can improve. I can use what I have learned to learn new things.*	Guidance and reflection	Observing, assess-ing through formal formative and perhaps some sum-mative procedures, measuring effective-ness of learning and application Planning next learning target and learning opportunities	Independent reading/ writing

Guiding Readers to Independence
by Erin Lucich

W hen I first began to implement guided reading, I'm quite sure I didn't understand it as an instructional approach. I would say, in fact, that if there was any instruction or learning happening, it was a happy accident. The focus for me was on "leveling" my readers, organizing them into groups based on these levels, and then helping them to problem-solve their way through a series of texts at the right level, hoping that soon they would graduate to the next level, where nothing would change except for the number or letter on the outside cover of the text. I understood that the role of the teacher was to support the reader through a text, my focus being absolutely on the **reading,** not the developing **reader.** The real outcome of my efforts was a classroom of readers who thought they needed me at every challenge point and a teacher (me) who was so overwhelmed by the needs that she felt, and often was, ineffective.

Things only began to change for me when I began to ask myself:

- What does it mean to guide a reader?

- Toward what am I guiding them?

- If guided reading is an instructional approach, then what am I instructing?

- What are these readers gaining or learning as a result of my instruction?

- Are these readers really leaving with anything beyond a new book that they can read?

Asking and beginning to answer these questions led me to redefine my role and responsibility as a teacher as well as the role and responsibility of a reader in a guided reading episode.

GUIDED READING IN A NUTSHELL

By the intermediate grades, readers generally have good decoding skills and are able to read most texts with accuracy. Understanding this, many teachers abandon guided reading as a practice, thinking of it as a tool to support a reader's accuracy, and therefore a technique most appropriate in the primary grades. However, readers of all ages need continuing instruction on how to process or navigate their way through increasingly difficult and varied texts while maintaining meaning and fluency. Guided reading is perhaps the most supportive context through which a learner can continue to build skills and strategies to cope with new and increasing demands on them as readers.

In a guided reading episode, the teacher accompanies readers as they interact with the authors and their messages, all the while supporting them toward specific learning outcomes. The teacher assists readers in recognizing their potential, helping them achieve what the teacher has assessed to be within their reach. As readers are closing in on their new learning, the teacher holds them accountable to use what they already know and encourages them to take new risks with what they are just beginning to understand.

Guided reading provides the teacher opportunity to extend the readers' knowing through limited and specific challenges in text. These challenges must be within reach for the readers, ensuring their sense of success and enjoyment, and therefore willingness to show up for the next experience. Identification of challenges results from the teacher's intentional assessment and matching of the reader and the text.[1] Instruction is built on strengths, so as readers build their knowledge base, the challenges should also increase, extending and stretching the readers.

SHIFTING FOCUS FROM CONTENT TO PROCESS: REACHING BEYOND THE TEXT

For many years the "reading process" (see Figure 5.1) was something that I thought of as generally applying to primary readers. When I taught primary grades, I looked at my reading observations through the lens of the reading process in order to understand the strategies readers were using and the sources of information (typically described as or broken down into meaning/semantic, structure/syntactical, and visual/phonological cues) that readers were responding to and using as they attempted to make meaning and

---

[1] *For support in analyzing texts for their instructional value so as to better match them to readers, consult Margaret Mooney's* A Book Is a Present: Selecting Text for Intentional Teaching *(2004).*

CAUGHT IN THE SPELL OF WRITING AND READING

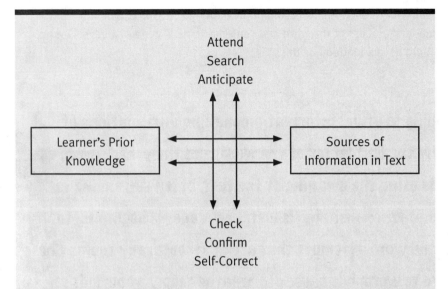

Strategies	
Attend	Pay particular attention to visual information
Search	Look purposefully for particular information
Anticipate	Predict alternatives or probabilities of text on the basis of prior knowledge and information in the text
Check	Reconsider response against more than one source of information
Confirm	Accept/reject the appropriateness of a response
Self-Correct	Provide an accurate response to the text in light of new information

Figure 5.1: The Reading Process
© 2005 by Richard C. Owen Publishers, Inc.

read with fluency. Analysis commonly didn't go beyond examination of the readers' process at the word and sentence level. A general analysis for me might have sounded like this:

This reader is attending to visual information, making anticipations of words using primarily the first letter of the word, and then checking to confirm her attempts using the meaning of the text, often re-reading to make another attempt when meaning is lost. The reader is beginning to check and reject initial word attempts that aren't structurally sound. She primarily reads word to word, but pauses to breathe deeply at periods and is beginning to recognize and read in phrases.

I would then use my analyses—the strengths and approximations of the readers—to identify learning outcomes and frame my guided reading lessons. Figure 5.2 contains a sampling of learning outcomes with corresponding questions that I might have used to support readers in moving through their process at the word and sentence level during a guided reading episode.

Sample Word and Sentence Level Process Outcomes	Sample Questions
Reader(s) will use structural cues to check to self-correct initial word attempts.	■ Does that sound right? ■ How do we say that? ■ How else might you say that? ■ What type of word is that?
Reader(s) will use meaning cues to check to confirm/reject initial word attempts.	■ Does that make sense? ■ What other words might make sense there?
Reader(s) will attend to the first letter sound to anticipate words.	■ What letter does that word start with? ■ What sound does it make?

Figure 5.2: Learning outcomes with corresponding questions for guided reading

CAUGHT IN THE SPELL OF WRITING AND READING

Once I moved up to support intermediate readers, there seemed less to analyze at the word and sentence level. While vocabulary development, knowledge of sound and word patterns, pace, phrasing, expression, and so on were still points of concern that needed to be attended to, there were larger comprehension issues that were unaccounted for in my analysis and so in my instruction. Understanding that comprehension was a huge concern, I began to focus my guided reading lessons primarily on the content of the texts being read. This focus was reflected in the questions that I asked readers before, during, and after reading:

- *Where did Jack and Jill go?*

- *Why did Jack and Jill go up the hill?*

- *What happened to Jack?*

Somewhere along the way I came to understand the difference between closed and open-ended questions. I began to shift my questions to be more open ended, believing that they would inspire more thinking and allow me to know more about my readers.

- *What do you think this text will be about?*

- *What's going to happen next?*

- *Who are the main characters?*

Yet my open-ended questions were still content oriented and solicited content-oriented reader responses. Focusing on the meaning of the text was generally easy, as it didn't necessarily require deeper analysis of readers' process or what it took for readers to gain meaning with particular texts. But because the focus was on content, I usually felt at a loss when readers lost meaning, most often swooping in to support them with the meaning of the text itself (the "what"), not with the meaning making (the "how" and "why").

I felt that what I was doing was resulting, at best, in accidental learning. I knew this because I was surprised every time readers indicated that they had learned something outside or beyond the content of the text. I had long been taking reading assessments that included listening to readers, recording what I heard, and asking and documenting their answers to content questions. But these assessments were of very limited use to me as a teacher, often only utilized to show reading level growth over time. I began to wonder more about **how** my readers were making meaning, feeling that if I could tap into their thinking, I might know how to shift my instruction to better impact their learning.

I knew that my content questions weren't really supporting the readers or giving me the information I needed, but I was finding it difficult to shift my questioning–to know what questions to ask to get to the thinking beyond the content. The fog began to lift when I started to use two general questions following each of my content questions: "How do you know?" and/or "What makes you think that?"

- *What do you think this text will be about? What makes you think that?*

- *What's going to happen next? How do you know?*

- *Who are the main characters? How do you know?*

These two questions solicited responses that revealed more than the readers' understandings or misunderstanding of content. I began to listen for the thinking or process of the reader, allowing me to feel like I could intentionally support the development of the reader and not just the reading for the first time. Figure 5.3 shows a sampling of typical reader responses to these questions.

What do you think this text will be about? What's going to happen next?	How do you know? What makes you think that?
"It's going to tell about all the different places animals hide."	"There are three different pictures that show three different places– ground, tree, and sand."
"The writer is going to try to convince us that Mr. Jones is the wrong candidate for president."	"This is an editorial, and because of the title I already know what the writer's position is."
"There's going to be some problem with Frankie. He's going to be a bad guy."	"When the writer says, 'Frankie was her friend, *or so she thought,*' I know that it means things are going to change."

Figure 5.3: Responses to questions focused on revealing the readers' thinking

As the readers continued to reveal bits of their thinking, I had a new challenge: I didn't know how to make sense of what I was hearing, which meant that I had difficulty probing and guiding the readers. I turned back to the reading process and began to reframe and extend my own understanding by thinking about application of this process at a broader level, what I now refer to as the "text level."

Through ongoing inquiry with my readers and examination of myself as a reader, I came to recognize that readers of all ages move through the same process. Readers continue to attend to, search, anticipate, check, confirm, and self-correct; and they continue to use what they know in response to the sources of information in text in order to make and maintain meaning and fluency. I realized that what was constantly changing and growing in sophistication and complexity were the sources of information in text that my readers were challenged to respond to.

As I worked through these increasingly difficult and changing sources of information in intermediate texts, I recognized that I could still describe them as meaning, structural, and visual cues, as shown in Figure 5.4.

	Meaning	Structure	Visual
Word/Sentence Level	Having to do with the meaning of specific words, word parts, and groups of words	Having to do with the grammatically sound construction of sentences	Having to do with letters and combinations of letters that make up words
Text Level	Having to do with the content and message of the larger text	Having to do with the form of the text, or genre	Having to do with the features in text, text type, and layout

Figure 5.4: Extending meaning, structural, and visual cues to the text level

I set about exploring and breaking down meaning, structural, and visual sources of information by thinking about the choices that writers make about which bits of information to include with respect to their chosen topic, purpose for writing, and intended audience, as laid out in Figure 5.5.

Building a window into the writer's thinking helped me to understand what readers needed to understand and be able to do and think about in order to interact with texts and authors. This growing discovery changed the way I assessed readers by bringing new depth to my thinking and listening, and ultimately changed the way that I attempted to support readers to new learning. Figure 5.6 is a sampling of learning outcomes with corresponding questions that I might use in a guided reading episode to both gather information and support readers in moving through their process in response to text-level sources of information.

Further understanding the reading process and the sources of information in text supported me both in knowing what questions to ask and being able to listen and make sense of the answers–the information the readers were

	Meaning	Structure	Visual
Text Level	Having to do with the content and message of the larger text	Having to do with the form of the text, or genre	Having to do with the features in text, text type, and layout
Examples of Choices Writers Make	■ Style ■ Topic ■ Theme ■ Language ■ Amount and type of detail ■ Word choice ■ Dialogue ■ Length ■ Mood ■ Content examples	■ Organization of ideas/ information ■ Character development ■ Sequence ■ Transitions ■ Style ■ Plot line ■ Language tense ■ Flow	■ Illustrations ■ Titles and subtitles ■ Cover information ■ Positioning of text ■ Font ■ Graphs ■ Tables ■ Captions ■ Labels

Figure 5.5: Examples of choices that writers make about information to include for their readers

giving me. Answers to these process questions gave me a window into the readers' thinking, allowing me to zero in on exactly what the reader did or didn't understand. And as I listened to what the readers were revealing to me, I was better able to flexibly intervene with specific questions and supports that would enable each reader to achieve new learning. My flexibility in responding to readers was absolutely an extension of my ability to listen and to make sense of what I was hearing.[2]

In the beginning, getting through the text itself had been the prize. Over time, developing the reader by **using** the text (even small pieces of it) became the prize. Shifting my focus from product to understanding and process enabled readers to access many texts (something that is increasingly important as learners progress through the grades), not just those that they read with me at their side. I by no means wish to imply that content isn't important, especially at the intermediate grades, but the real challenge for the teacher in developing readers is finding ways to enable readers to access many texts and many pieces of content, not just the few texts or slices of content that they are able to work through with the teacher at their side.

---

[2] For further support in understanding and breaking down the choices authors make related to text forms (structure) and features (visual), consult Margaret Mooney's Text Forms and Features: A Resource for Intentional Teaching (2001).

Sample Text Level Process Outcomes	Sample Questions
Related to meaning: Reader(s) will understand how to use what they know about same and similar topics to make, check, and change predictions throughout their reading.	■ What do you know about _____? What do you know about that's similar to _____? How might this knowledge support you as a reader? ■ How did you learn about _____? What might that tell you about the choices this writer might make in revealing _____ to you through this text? What type of reading and thinking might you have to do? ■ What are you thinking now? Does this match what you thought at the outset? How has your thinking changed?
Related to structure: Reader(s) will understand the general characteristics of a persuasive letter and begin to use their understandings to make anticipations before heading into their reading.	■ What does it mean to persuade somebody? ■ Who is the target audience for this piece? ■ How might the author attempt to influence your thinking? What does this mean for you as a reader? What kind of thinking will you have to do? ■ What's the shape of a persuasive letter? How is it like or unlike other letters? How might this help you as a reader? ■ In what other forms might an author write to persuade? Why might an author choose a letter over the other forms? ■ What does the author expect of you in return? ■ What kind of language and techniques might you expect?
Related to visual: Reader(s) will understand the qualities of a map and how and when to use it as a source of information within a larger text.	■ What is a map? ■ What purpose does it serve for the author? The reader? ■ When might you look to maps? ■ In what forms of text might you find them? Where might the author place them as part of a text? Why? ■ How does an author relate information through a map?

Figure 5.6: Learning outcomes with corresponding questions for guided reading

WE'VE GOT THE PROCESS; NOW WHAT?

In a guided reading episode, the job of the teacher is to support learners with the thinking they need in order to put new learning/understandings to work for them as they read. This thinking/process is guided or facilitated by the questions that teachers ask. Teachers must be ever mindful of the readers' capabilities–of what they know and are able to do as well as what is within their reach–or there's risk of fostering dependence on the teacher to facilitate readers through every challenge point. And the ultimate prize is reader independence, not dependence.

Guided reading is the process of releasing responsibility for the question asking onto the readers, outfitting them with the questions they need to facilitate their own process independently. Whether we're talking about word, sentence, or text level processing, it's the questions that reflect understanding and process that support independence. In other words, independence is the ability of learners to ask their own process questions and the action of the learners resulting from their answers.

It took some time for me to realize that my support of independence, the release of the questioning, could and should be intentional, even systematic. I came to a point when I felt good about the quality and depth of the learning resulting from my guided reading instruction, but I began to notice that readers weren't making much use of what they had learned in their independent work.

I began to see better results in the transfer of student learning to independence by making some very intentional shifts in my practice:

- As a part of my planning, I began to write down the questions related to each learning outcome that I hoped readers would leave with. (Often these questions would change a bit. Anticipation of what these questions **could** sound like is what made the difference.)

- I charted these questions during guided reading and encouraged readers to ask themselves and each other the questions during and after each teaching episode.

- I began to make sure that there was ample opportunity within the guided reading episode for the readers to approximate–to begin to apply the learning independently.

- I wrapped up each learning episode by asking the readers, "What have you learned? What does this mean for you as a reader? What other learning or understandings can you connect this to?"

RECORD OF LEARNING

Name: _____   Date(s): _____

Date	New Learning	Thinking	Evidence	Date
(Goal Set)	■ *What do I now understand?*	■ *What does this mean for me as a reader?* ■ *What will I be asking myself?*	■ *How will I know that I'm making progress?* ■ *What will be the result of this change in thinking?*	(Goal Observed)

Figure 5.7: Record of Learning
Form © 2006 by Erin Lucich

■ I began to better anticipate what the evidence of student learning would be–how the students and I would monitor their learning during and after the lessons.

■ I started to use a Record of Learning (Figure 5.7) on which the readers recorded their new learning/understandings, the questions that they felt would assist them in shifting their own thinking and doing, and the evidence that would support them (and me) in assessing their movement toward their goal.

Over time, the questioning and answering started to become automatic for my students. They began to better understand and be able to articulate their own strengths, challenges, goals, what it would take to achieve those goals, and how they would monitor the shifts in their own learning. They began to take new pride and ownership in their learning and were better prepared to work independently. This freed me up to monitor for learning instead of trouble-shooting and to meet with individuals and groups.

GENERALIZING KNOWING:
THE READER-WRITER CONNECTION

For me, the "link" between reading and writing often came after a guided reading lesson and was merely a written response or interpretation of the content of the text read. While I was in fact getting the students to write, I began to wonder whether it was doing anything, in a long-lasting sense, for the writers and their development.

I, like so many teachers, have often felt overwhelmed by the demands of the job and the limited time given to carry them out. When I began to think about maximizing student learning, I found an added benefit of shifting my readers' learning goals from product focused to process focused. I discovered that outcomes that reach beyond the content of a text and into the reader's understanding and process are easy to generalize across content, setting, and situation ("easy" compared to product or content outcomes that are difficult, if not impossible, to generalize). Generalization of learning most certainly needs to be supported, but the potential for it exists, rooted in what the learner now knows and is able to do.

If learning goes beyond the content and into the understanding and process of the reader, the "link" to the writer can be found in an alternate application of the learning. For example, if a reader understands the techniques that authors use to influence their thinking as they read a persuasive text, they may be better equipped to use these techniques as they attempt to persuade readers through their own writing. Furthermore, the process questions that readers ask can be easily translated into questions writers ask themselves as they write. For example, the reader's question, "How might the author attempt to influence my thinking?" translates into, "How will I influence my readers' thinking?" for the writer.

To be clear, any application of learning must be supported over time, but the planting of the seed can come easily by using the text as a model for the writer, helping the reader to connect with the thinking of the writer behind the text. I found that by asking a few simple questions during and after a guided reading lesson, I could at the very least set the stage for the writer's future approximation:

- *What does this learning mean for you as a writer?*

- *How might these questions translate into questions that might support you as a writer?*

- *What kind of thinking did this author do here? What choices did she make?*

- *What does this author understand?*

I also began to trial a new Record of Learning (Figure 5.8) that supported me and my learners in automatically thinking about how learning might link across content areas.

RECORD OF LEARNING

Name: _____   Date(s): _____

New Learning	Thinking as a Reader...	Evidence	Date	Thinking as a Writer...	Evidence	Date
■ What do I now understand?	■ What does this mean for me as a reader? ■ What will I be asking myself?	■ How will I know that I'm making progress? ■ What will be the result of this change in thinking?	(Observed)	■ What does this mean for me as a writer? ■ What will I be asking myself?	■ How will I know that I'm making progress? ■ What will be the result of this change in thinking?	(Observed)

Figure 5.8: Record of Learning supporting the reader-writer connection

Form © 2006 by Erin Lucich

With the introduction of this form (as well as with the original Record of Learning in Figure 5.7), I was able to check that the conversation had gone beyond content, for it was near impossible to ask and answer the questions on the new Record of Learning if the dialogue had never reached beyond content. It also supported me in beginning to think about how learning could be generalized to other content areas, such as math and science. I began to see that "beyond content" learning had benefits for reader to reader, reader to writer, reader to mathematician, writer to reader, writer to mathematician, scientist to reader, and so on. I began to understand that instructional outcomes in general, just by the mere fact that they reached deeply enough, extended the invitation to the learner to generalize, bridge, and connect pieces of their learning.

Planning

PUTTING IT TOGETHER

At one time, my planning for guided reading basically consisted of a reference to a list of student reading levels and a rather random selection of appropriately leveled text. But as I grew in my understanding, everything changed. I began to ask myself important questions as I prepared for teaching, such as:

- What do I want these readers to understand and be able to do?

- Who is close to this understanding/doing?

- What do they already know that will support them toward new learning? What strengths can be drawn upon?

- Will the dynamics of the group support learning? What strengths will the different players bring? What will be the challenges?

- What resource(s) or part of the resource(s) will appeal to the readers and also challenge them toward the learning outcome(s)?

- Where in the text can I anticipate that readers will need more support?

- Where are the opportunities in this text to support readers toward the outcome(s)?

- Where in the text do I want readers to spend more time talking, searching, discovering, and so on? How will I set the stage for that?

- Will I use the whole text or just parts?

- How will I provide support toward the outcome, yet still encourage reader responsibility and independence?

■ Where/when might I guide? Where/when might I be able to step back and let them go it alone?

■ What kinds of questions will I ask? What questions do I want readers to leave asking?

■ What action of the reader will result from the question asking? What will the evidence of learning be? What are the anticipated shifts in behavior resulting from the shift in understanding?

■ What are the opportunities for generalization of learning? How will I support the readers in linking knowledge?

■ Where, when, and how do I expect them to practice? What resources will support further application of this learning?

■ How and when will we (student and teacher) monitor as learning is being acquired? As learning is being applied? When will we check in?

As I attempted to shift my own behavior in planning for learning, I wrote a lot of notes to myself in my lesson plans and on self-stick notes that I placed in texts. Over time, as my thinking became more automatic, I found that I didn't need as many notes-to-self. And, although the thinking I did in preparation for my teaching only grew and expanded, I began only to need a few basic notes in my lesson plans (Figure 5.9) to support me in my guided reading lessons.

GUIDED READING PLANS

Date: _____ Students: _____ Outcome: _____ Questions: _____ _____ Resource: _____	Date: _____ Students: _____ Outcome: _____ Questions: _____ _____ Resource: _____
Date: _____ Students: _____ Outcome: _____ Questions: _____ _____ Resource: _____	Date: _____ Students: _____ Outcome: _____ Questions: _____ _____ Resource: _____

Figure 5.9: A framework for planning

I understand now that planning needs to be every bit as intentional as the instruction itself. And, although one cannot anticipate all that it will take in order for learning to occur, it is the anticipations that provide footing for the teacher, starting blocks from which they can flexibly proceed toward student learning.

Teaching

Picture this: The teacher sits at a round table with six students. They sit comfortably in the corner of the room next to a small sign that the teacher has posted reading, "Please do not disturb. If you have a concern or question that only I can support you with, feel free to write me a note and post it here." The teacher is positioned so that she can glance up periodically to monitor the goings-on in the classroom. The other students in the classroom are reading and writing independently, with their Record of Learning forms out and in front of them. The room is not silent. Though many students are working silently, several small groups of students are talking in low voices about their reading and writing.

Because she is introducing something new, the teacher plans to meet with this small group for approximately 25 minutes. She has her lesson plans in front of her, along with a chart pad and a stack of six books, one copy for each student at the table. Her lesson plans read:

Date: **5-10-05**

Students: **Jared, Marcy, Eli, Lucas, Cory, Sophie**

Outcome: **Students will understand the purposes and characteristics of an editorial in order to make good anticipations about the text and the kind of thinking they need to be doing from the onset.**

Questions:

- **What does/might this writer want me to think?**

- **How might the writer attempt to influence my thinking?**

- **What is expected of me as the reader of editorials?**

- **What kind of thinking might I have to do?**

Resource: **(a nonfiction magazine for kids)**

Figure 5.10: Sample lesson plan

The teacher begins the lesson by touching on the learners' previous learning:

- *"We're sort of making the transition to new territory today, but I still want to connect with you again about your learning since we last met. Boy, I sure heard some great thinking from you all this week when I checked in. Anyone care to share?*

- *"Where have you shown/seen evidence of your growth?*

- *"I saw Eli sharing his writing with Riley. Were you able to do some new trialing there? Would you like to share a bit with the group?"*

The teacher begins to set the stage for a new line of study.

"Today we're going to be learning about editorials so that we can make good anticipations, or predictions, about the kind of thinking we need to be doing as readers of editorials. I've posted some guiding questions that we'll be using as we work through this learning:

- *What does/might this writer want me to think?*

- *How might the writer attempt to influence my thinking?*

- *What is expected of me as the reader of editorials?*

- *What kind of thinking might I have to do?"*

The teacher proceeds:

"We'll come back to these questions in a moment, but for now let me ask you:

- *What do you know about the role of an editor?*

- *If they have final say about what should go in and what should be cut, and most likely make their choices based on their position or where they want to guide their readers' thinking, then what do you suppose an editorial is? An editor's note?"*

The teacher records reader responses to these questions on a piece of chart paper that says, "What?" at the top.

She then asks:

- *"For what purpose do you suppose they might be written?*

- *Why and when might someone choose to write one?"*

The teacher asks a few more guiding questions specific to reader responses and then records their responses on a piece of chart paper that says, "Why & When?" at the top.

The teacher continues:

- *"Looking at the title of this piece, what would you guess this editor's position or opinion to be?*

- *Do you believe it to be a strongly held position, one that he might be intense about or about which he might be quite convincing? What makes you think that? Read the title again. What language does this writer use to let you know exactly how passionate he is?*

- *What else on the page can help you to confirm that?*

- *So if he's writing with passion, do you suppose he'll stop with just sharing his opinion or viewpoint, or will he want you right there with him? How do you suppose he might go about attempting to persuade, influence, or convince you?"*

The teacher begins to record reader responses to these questions on a piece of chart paper that says, "How?" at the top. She continues to record reader responses to the following questions:

- *"Do you suppose he will come right out and tell you what he wants you to think? What would that sound like?*

- *What if he doesn't want to come right out and tell you, but maybe wants to make good point after good point, giving hint after hint through the telling of 'his story' or the way 'he sees it' until he's got you thinking just as he hoped? What could that sound like? How might he do that?*

- *I think about it as the difference between a direct hit and an indirect hit. So Cory and Sophie, you play soccer. . . Are there times when you shoot directly for the goal? When do you do that? Are there times when you have to play your moves a little more in order to fake the other players out? When do you have to do that? How do you do that?*

■ *Think about the other players as the writer's audience. When might he be able or want to shoot straight for the goal? When might he want or need to play his moves? How might he do that? What techniques might he use?*

■ *How will you be able to tell the difference between a direct and indirect hit? What will you have to do and think about from the get-go in order to tell the difference? With which strategy will you have to think harder?*

■ *Do you suppose he'll share the **whole** story with you? What type of information might he choose to include? What might he choose to leave out?"*

The teacher draws the students' attention to a chart labeled, "So what?" and asks:

■ *"So, what does all of this mean for you as readers of this text?*

■ *What kind of thinking will you have to do throughout this reading? How will you organize your thinking inside your head?*

■ *And what will you have to make up your own mind about? How will you do that? Will it happen right away?"*

The teacher probes and charts reader responses, then proceeds to set a task:

■ *"As you're reading this text the first time through, I want you to think about whether or not this writer is attempting to convince you of something, and if he is, I want you to think about how he's going about that from beginning to end."*

As she's assigning this task, the teacher refers back to the "Why & When?" chart to support readers in thinking about the possible purposes of this piece of text, and then to the "How?" chart to support readers in thinking about the characteristics of the text and potential techniques that may be used by the writer. The teacher also points to the "Guiding Questions" chart paper, starring the first two questions listed:

■ What does this writer want me to think?

■ How might the writer attempt to influence my thinking?

The group reads through the short text, commenting as they confirm their anticipations about it. The teacher proceeds with the following questions, recording new thoughts on the "How?" chart, as well as confirming some previously stated thoughts by starring them.

- *"What techniques did the writer use? What language? What examples?*

- *How did the writer make you feel? How did he achieve that?*

- *Was he direct or indirect?"*

The teacher then refers to the "So what?" chart and stars the second two questions listed on the "Guiding Questions" chart:

- What is expected of me as the reader?

- What kind of thinking might I have to do?

The teacher asks:

- *"How much of the story do you suppose you got? What will you do to fill in the missing pieces of the story? Do you need to fill in the missing pieces of the story? How might you do that? If not now, when might you need to do that? Why?*

- *So what kind of thinking did you have to do?"*

The teacher begins to support students to closure, asking them to record their responses to the following questions on their Records of Learning (Figure 5.11), which at this point in the year they are quite comfortable doing:

- *"So what would you say you learned today?*

- *What does that mean for you as readers?*

- *What questions will you be asking yourselves?*

- *And what will the result be? How will you know that you're making progress?"*

The teacher supports the students in beginning to link this learning to their writing:

- *"Now let's think for a minute about what this learning means or could mean for you as writers.*

- *Jared, you were talking about that new video game the other day. How might you go about convincing your folks that it's an appropriate*

RECORD OF LEARNING

Name: _____ Date(s): _____

New Learning	Thinking as a Reader...	Evidence	Date	Thinking as a Writer...	Evidence	Date
What do I now understand?	What does this mean for me as a reader? What will I be asking myself?	How will I know that I'm making progress? What will be the result of this change in thinking?	(Observed)	What does this mean for me as a writer? What will I be asking myself?	How will I know that I'm making progress? What will be the result of this change in thinking?	(Observed)
–Editorials are meant to influence the readers' thinking. –The author uses specific techniques in order to do this. –The reader gets to make an informed decision about what they believe.	–What does the writer want me to think? –How might they try to influence my thinking? –What kind of thinking do I have to do as I read? In response to the reading?	–I will not believe everything I read. –I will be able to make an informed decision for myself. –I will know where to look to understand the writer's position, and what they WANT me to believe. –I will search for answers to unanswered questions and missing information.		–What do I want my readers to think? –How will I influence their thinking? What techniques will I use? –How will I get them to think like me?	–I will use tools and techniques to make sure that I'm convincing—I'll have readers thinking just like me!	

Figure 5.11: Sample Record of Learning
Form © 2006 by Erin Lucich

choice for you? What would make or break the argument? What do they really care about?

■ *So if Jared were to write an editorial for the purpose not just of stating his opinion, but of convincing his parents (or all parents) of the appropriateness of that video game, what information might he choose to include and what might he choose to leave out? And would he go for a direct hit or would he need to be playing some moves? How might that sound?*

■ *So what questions can you be asking yourselves as writers?*

■ *What will be the result? How will you know that you're making progress?"*

The students record their thinking on their own Records of Learning (see Figure 5.11).

Continuing, the teacher states:

■ *"In the next couple of weeks we'll be adding to our thinking about the purposes for writing editorials and the techniques and choices writers make. We'll also be connecting this to other forms of writing that may have similar purposes and characteristics.*

■ *So, in order to continue our conversation, here is a selection of editorials. Over the next couple of days, until we meet again, I want you to be thinking about the questions here on your Records of Learning. I also want you to add to, question, or challenge any of the thoughts we have on our charts as you learn more about what editorials are, why and when they're written, how authors make choices about what and how to include information, and what it all means for us as readers and writers. I'll post the charts here on the wall so that you'll have easy access."*

Throughout the lesson, it is clear that each question the teacher has asked has been influenced by the responses of her students. It is also evident that students are growing in their level of understanding and in their ability to make use of what they are learning to move through their process, using questions to frame their thinking.

Monitoring the Learning

Shifts in learner understanding should result in shifts in learner behavior. These shifts in behavior can be anticipated in order that the teacher and student can monitor the learning over time. Thinking about how the learning will be evidenced (and even documenting it) makes the learning concrete and supports the teacher and student in knowing what to look and listen for.

The Record of Learning is one example of a documentation tool that can support both the teacher and the student in ongoing monitoring of learning, generalization of learning, connection between pieces of learning, and celebration of learning. Another tool that has proven to be very helpful for use in conjunction with the Record of Learning is a simple sheet of mailing labels (approximately one label for each learner) that can be carried around on a teacher clipboard. The teacher can anticipate and record evidence of individual learning during teaching episodes, during students' independent work time, during analysis of classroom assessments, and so on. The teacher can also record any new information and wonderings about learners. This information can be used for future planning, and then, when the teacher is "finished" with the information, the labels can be peeled off, placed in a notebook under individual student names, and used as a summary of each student's learning over time.

Once upon a time I took notes and records because I thought I was supposed to. It didn't matter that I recorded completely random observations, because quantity and frequency of note-taking was how I measured my success. These days I'm not as concerned with the quantity, frequency, or tool as I am with the usefulness of the information to me and to my students. I now value assessments only to the extent that they help me to do my job and the students to do theirs.

I believe that knowing and being able to support readers is entirely dependent on the shape of the teacher's understanding and their willingness to continue their own growth and learning through inquiry and reflection. Over time I've become quite confident (but not always comfortable with the idea) that there is no "there" there; that this is an ever-evolving learning process. At times this can be fantastically frustrating, but what keeps me going is the growing ease with which I'm able to apply my understandings across content, setting, and situation; the promise of new learning; and the inevitable benefits of my growing understanding on student learning.

Guiding Writers to Independence

by Margaret E. Mooney

CHAPTER

6

Six sixth-grade students and the teacher are gathered around a group of tables. The students have their writing books, a pen, and a pencil. The teacher has a sketchpad and a marker. The sketchpad is open, displaying the group learning goal.

> **Our current learning is checking that our texts have a definite conclusion—a resolution, a summary, or a thought-provoking statement.**

A pile of dictionaries is on the table. The remainder of the class is working on writing tasks. Some are working in pairs, revising and editing their work; others are either composing a piece or working on a presentation for publication. Two students are working at the computer. The following excerpts are from the twenty minutes the teacher spent with the group at the table. During this time she moves to the center of the room once, saying in a quiet voice, *"Relax, writers. Pens down for a minute. Draw breath. Think about what you have done. Is it as you want it to be? Read to check and then resume work. I'm looking forward to seeing and hearing what you have achieved."* The teacher talks to three students to get them to refocus on their work. She then returns to the group at the table. There is a quiet hum during the twenty minutes, and a few students do move from their desks, but no one interrupts the group.

> T: *Before we talk about beginning a new piece of work, re-read your last piece. Think about your personal goal for that piece. Put a mark in the margin where you think you achieved that goal. Now do the same for our group target. Take a few minutes and share these celebratory pieces.*

There's a lively exchange between group members. Some of the other students sitting within earshot stop writing to listen. The teacher watches and listens.

S: Hey! You need to hear this bit!

The group stops to listen as one student reads a few sentences. There's affirmation from the group.

T: *I can see why you wanted us all to hear that piece. I think you should indicate that is a benchmark for you to use in your next piece. Now let's think about today's learning. First think about our group goal. Are we there yet?*

The students chat among themselves for a couple of minutes before coming to a consensus that further work is required.

T: *Let's review what we have done so far to help us with our goal.*

The students refer to the three pieces written during the past week.

T: *What do we know that can help us develop a tight and appropriate ending?*

S: Well, like you said, a good plan.

S: Putting your strongest argument at the end.

T: *Keep going – in order to. . .?*

S: It will lead naturally into a good conclusion.

S: Not including any similes or chances for the reader to question you– that's in a persuasive text.

S: And it works for expository.

S: You have to make the reader know you know what you are talking about.

S: I'm going to put my introduction at the end and then write a new introduction.

T: *It might be a good idea to test that out on one of the pieces you have already written.*

S: I am trying to strike a good sentence length. It can't be too long, but short sentences don't work at the end either.

S: It's best to end with your own words rather than someone else's.

T: *These are all good. So why are you finding it so challenging to end your pieces of expository or persuasive writing with a tight ending that goes beyond your introduction? What have we agreed is the most important criteria when writing to convince or persuade someone? Won't that also help you with a focused ending?*

S: Know your topic well.

S: Don't write it unless you are sure.

S: Or can make it look as if you are.

The teacher has recorded the ideas on the sketch pad:

Know your topic

Rehearse before you write

Convince your reader

T: *I think you also need to think about the layout of your plan. If you are using a graphic organizer, you need to check that it really suits the structure of your piece and that it includes a prime position for pulling everything together. Josie, I noticed the graphic organizer you were using for a cause and effect structure for your piece persuading the school board to get new stage curtains was like this. I think you would find it helpful to show your key idea and then have a summary box for just one word or phrase from each and then bring it down to your conclusion. You might like to try that in your planning.*

Can we agree we'll work on another persuasive piece and we'll consider these points as we plan for a summary ending that takes the reader beyond what they brought to the piece? Make sure you have made a good topic choice, think about the kind of thinking you want your reader to do, make your plan reflect that, and then draft your plan ready for a discussion before you get into your piece. Remember, conclusions don't just happen. They can take as long and as much effort as the sum of the rest of the piece.

S: Can it be a negative piece about something we don't like? You can feel strongly about that.

T: *Good idea, and I think I can predict what your topic might be! Before you begin writing your plan, check that you have at least three strong reasons to support your stance.*

. . .

Once you have your topic, think about your personal goal. What are you working to improve?

As the students settle to work, the teacher chats with each one. They discuss topics and possible planning structures, with the teacher giving reminders to think about the conclusion at the planning stage. The remainder of the lesson is devoted to the students working on their plans. The teacher talks with each student, making suggestions, asking questions, listening, and watching. The students chat among themselves from time to time. The lesson concludes with a sharing of plans. The teacher draws their attention to the sketch pad:

T: *How many of these criteria supported your planning? Can we add anything to our list of supports?*

S: I'm going to end with a question, as you did when you showed us your piece about culling elephants in Africa.

T: *See how it works. Remember we are trying several options rather than saying there is a formula. Do you have sufficient planning done so you can continue working on your own tomorrow?*

SOME ESSENTIAL ELEMENTS OF A GUIDED WRITING SESSION

As I reflect on this lesson, I am reminded of the following elements I consider among those essential when using the guided approach to assist writers who have already acquired some basic strategies:

- Continuous commitment to learning

- Working toward manageable personal and group goals

- Continued development of self-monitoring and self-improving strategies through self assessment

- Working persistently to overcome challenges

- Choice with responsibility

- Being a responsible group member, learning from and contributing to the learning of others.

The guided approach builds on the foundations that teachers establish during shared writing, when they explicitly demonstrate the thinking that writers employ when planning, shaping, and recording ideas and information. Students are encouraged to emulate these thinking patterns as they practice and refine their understandings and skills within the supportive though expectant context of a guided session. I once described the guided approach as flying solo under supervision. Despite some refinements in practice, I still consider that this brief definition should underscore how students perceive their role.

By Grade 3, students should have a clear understanding of the responsibilities and benefits of being a group member, and they should capitalize on the opportunity to further their learning. The small group context, common in most guided sessions, affords one-on-one time with the teacher and an audience and support network of writers of a similar developmental level. This means that each student has instant and continuous access to someone able to listen, question, assist, and challenge at a comparable level, nurturing honesty and trust. Of course, this support works two ways, allowing each student to reciprocate and learn from the experiences and work of other group members.

If the student's role is flying solo under supervision, the teacher's role is one of keeping the plane aloft through a watchful and supervisory eye. The effectiveness of guided writing is dependent on the teacher's understanding of:

- The role of the written word within society

- The part reading and writing play in her own life, and her competence as a writer in the forms, styles, and content in which she will provide instruction and support and will assess

- What skills, content, and standards are negotiable and what are required

- Each student's attitude, learning style, competencies, experiences of the world and of writing, and interests

- The developmental stages of learning and of learning reading and writing

- The role and nature of intentional and differentiated instruction

- The interdependence of the modes of language

- The range of functions, forms and styles, skills, and strategies that the students will require during the year

- Resources available to support instruction.

The effectiveness of guided writing is also dependent on the teacher's ability to:

- Create a trusting climate within the class and within each group

- Share the benefits of being a writer

The Student's Role Is Flying Solo under Supervision

The Teacher's Role Is Keeping the Plane Aloft

- Identify manageable learning targets and relevant learning opportunities

- Motivate each student to be continuously engaged with learning

- Prompt and provoke each student to practice and refine skills and strategies already in place and those currently being acquired

- Continuously monitor each student's application to the task and to new learning

- Provide immediate and individual feedback relevant to the learning target

- Encourage a self-monitoring and self-improving routine within each student

- Maintain a classroom environment and program that allows for regular uninterrupted guided sessions and meaningful independent experiences.

Guided Writing Warrants as Much Attention as Guided Reading

Guided writing has not received the same attention as guided reading despite the commonalities between the two language modes that, when acknowledged and made explicit to students, bring economy and depth to learning. Reading and writing are both key to learning in all content curriculum. They are both central to much of the assessment of a student's progress beyond Grade 3. Writing is evidence of a student's ability to transfer much of the learning gained through instruction and practice in reading. Skills listed in the reading sections of state and district scope-and-sequence documents are very similar, if not the same, as those in documents for writing instruction and assessment. And writing development requires the same passionate and intensive nurturing as reading requires and receives.

However, this is not the reality. The results of several informal but extensive surveys of teachers concur that more time is devoted to planning reading than given to writing; teachers express a concern that students read for pleasure but referred to writing as being mainly to complete assignments; and there is agreement that there are more remedial programs focused on assisting students experiencing reading difficulties than for struggling or overwhelmed writers. There are other discrepancies between attention paid to instruction and resources devoted to the two modes, but those listed are closely aligned to the guided approach. But one that cannot be omitted is the distinction in assessment. Much of the assessment of reading is formative with continuous or, at the very least, regular monitoring of a student's progress with instant feedback and support. In contrast, much of the assessment of writing, while frequent, is summative, with feedback after a red pen postmortem and either a rating or peripheral comment.

When teachers completing the surveys were asked why writing received less attention, resources, planning, and enthusiasm than reading, the most common answers were about the number of skills to be taught or amount of the marking. (Some issues concerning marking will be discussed later in this chapter.) It is easy for teachers in middle and upper grades to be overwhelmed by the number of skills listed in state and district documents as required teaching at these levels. Economy and effectiveness of instruction can be enhanced when time is taken to identify skills and strategies common to reading and writing as well as those introduced in some form prior to the student's current grade. This knowledge, along with critical and current information about each student's competencies and experiences, will shape all stages of planning.

PLANNING

Effective planning requires knowing the school year's required coverage. If a program or a specific set of resources is used, long-term planning needs to ensure that it is totally congruent with state and district requirements. If it is not, supplementary resources and instruction need to be included in planning at this stage. Long-term plans outlining required coverage for a year or certainly a term are usually developed by the whole staff of a school or at least some staff representatives. However they are developed, it is each teacher's responsibility to be thoroughly conversant with the contents and to use these as the backbone for planning, especially when considering the focus of guided writing as the central instructional approach.

Long-term Planning Shows Coverage of Skills and Strategies

Once the year's scope and sequence has been determined, the teacher can take a medium-term view, identifying the rhythm and pace of coverage for each group of students. Medium-term planning for guided writing allows the teacher to select a sequence and range of appropriate and manageable instructional opportunities while, at the same time, utilizing opportunities to provide practice and further instruction in other curriculum areas. Being realistic about the range of students (which could be as wide as five years) and cognizant of skills common to reading and writing and to more than one grade level or curriculum area is critical at this stage, when differentiated instruction needs to be planned.

Medium-term Planning Identifies Opportunities for Differentiated Instruction

One of the ways differentiated instruction can be implemented is through grouping students to narrow the range. Options for the composition of groups include common need (for example, skills or attitude), interests, mixed ability, developmental stage, student choice, or using the same groups for writing as for reading. While the advantages and disadvantages of each type of group make it prudent to change from time to time, I usually prefer to keep the same group for writing as for reading in order to optimize links between reading and writing. "You learned it from an author, now let's use it as an author" is one way of making the links overt. Also, keeping the same grouping for reading and writing makes for ease of management for both teacher and students, especially if the literacy block includes both guided reading and writing. Whatever grouping is used, I believe the main–and for me, the only–criterion for the guided approach should be to enable every student to make a continuous commitment to learning that promotes continuous progress through manageable challenges of increasing complexity.

Details of Instruction and Monitoring Are Key to Short-term Planning

The nature and dynamics of the group will influence the ease with which specific skills and content acquired during the reading of certain texts can be incorporated into instruction and references made to specific examples and techniques during guided sessions. This becomes the focus of short-term planning, when continuous monitoring of each student's work determines the pace of implementation of the longer plans. Long-term planning and medium-term planning are concerned with the learning and what students are able to do as a result of the learning. Short-term planning requires consideration of the students' most recent reading and writing experiences when selecting a written activity as the vehicle for further instruction and learning through guided writing. As each lesson is planned, consideration should be given to the degree that each student is meeting the success criteria identified at the commencement of each unit.

Fundamental to a successful guided lesson is the student's ability to initiate and sustain commitment to a task. This means that the majority of guided writing sessions should require students to be involved in a range of opportunities that provoke the recording of ideas and information. When all aspects of prompts are given, the writing becomes an assignment and not a learning activity. All effort and focus is on delivering what is required and not on what is possible or what could be learned through "exploring with the pen." If students are always given a complete set of parameters, they will not see writing as a pleasurable activity of choice and one they can use for their own purposes or in their own style. Developing one's individual voice or voices–for skilled writers are able to engage their readers through a variety of styles and tones–is an area of critical learning once the basics of writing have been mastered. For this reason I do not follow the practice of writing formulas, such as:

topic + audience + purpose = form.

I much prefer students to understand that any one of those could be the point of entry to the process, as shown in Figure 6.1. Whichever are the "givens" need to be complemented by the others, and at these middle and upper grades students need an awareness that the combination of these elements will determine the writing style employed.

The listing of topic, theme, and issue instead of just topic is important, for these three levels of thinking and recording are essential to learning in all

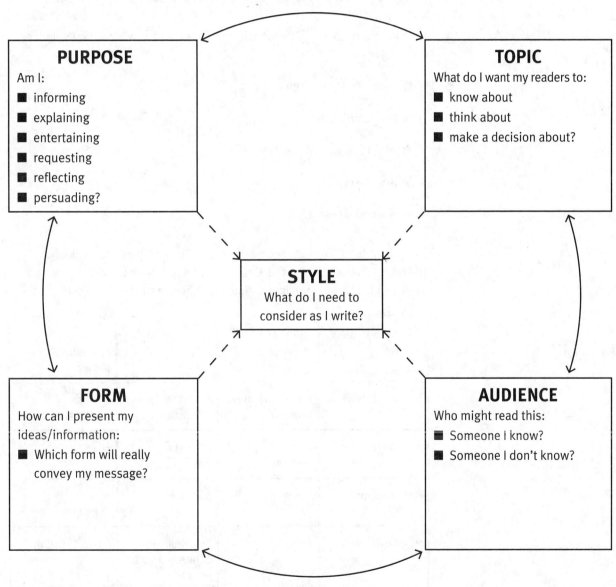

Figure 6.1: Different entry points to planning for writing
© 2006 by Margaret E. Mooney

curriculum areas beyond Grade 3. The thinking required for these levels is comparable to literal, inferential, and analytical comprehension in reading and, in their most simplistic form, may be introduced to student writers as:

What do you want you readers to know? What are you going to tell them? (Topic)

What do you want your readers to think about? What are you going to leave for them to fill in or add to our words? (Theme)

What do you want your readers to choose or make a decision about? (Issue).

The effectiveness of any lesson will be influenced by each student's understanding of:

■ How letters and sounds work

■ How words work

■ How language works

■ How texts work

■ How books work.

These understandings are recorded here as students need to think about and understand them. Teachers attach labels with both the descriptor and emphasis changing from time to time, as shown in the chart in Figure 6.2.

How sounds and letters work	Alphabetic principle	Phonological	Phonemic Awareness Phonics
How words work	Language code Grammar	Phonological Syntactic	Phonics Vocabulary
How language works	Grammar Meaning	Syntactic Semantic	Fluency
How texts work	Meaning	Semantic	Fluency Comprehension
How books work	Meaning	Semantic Concepts about print	Comprehension

Figure 6.2: Understandings about language needed by all students

Increasing each student's competence in all of these five areas should underpin every guided writing lesson. For example, a lesson intended to increase
students' use of alliteration to provide detail and cause readers to create
images in their head is dependent on each writer's knowledge of sound and
letter patterns, repertoire of oral and aural vocabulary, understanding of
grammar to select the correct word function and of the sequence that en-
genders the desired impact within the reader, and commitment and respect
for the content and the reader. While any one of these components may be
highlighted momentarily within the instruction, none can stand alone within
the context of writing–and of writing at all levels of competency and in any
and all forms and styles. The five essentials of phonemic awareness, phonics,
vocabulary, fluency, and comprehension are not limited to reading or to the
early grades, but are the foundation of the most skilled writer's toolbox, as
shown in the chart in Figure 6.3.

Phonemic awareness	Alliteration Onomatopoeia Assonance Syllabification
Phonics	Spelling Affixes Rhyme Rhythm Homographs, homonyms, and homophones
Vocabulary	Content area vocabularies Assignment and test vocabularies Vocabulary of technology Book language and poetic vocabulary Contemporary and historical vocabularies Synonyms and antonyms Derivatives
Fluency	Phrases and clauses Punctuation Sentences and paragraphs

Comprehension	Text forms and features
	Presenting material for ease of ac-
	    cessing intended meaning and
	    emphasis
	Intrinsic rewards

Figure 6.3: The five essentials–the foundation of the most skilled writer's toolbox

In the same way, if the "six traits of writing" are forming a framework for the student's writing, instruction in any one needs to be embedded in consideration of how it affects and is affected by the other five. All six need to be understood from the writer's and the reader's perspectives and linked to other elements of writing instruction. For example:

Content

Vocabulary, fluency, and comprehension:

The writer's perspective (shown in roman type throughout this section)

What ideas and/or information do I want to present to my readers?

What do I want my readers to know, think, or decide? (Topic, theme and issue)

The reader's perspective (shown in italics throughout this section)

What is the author telling me? What does the author want me to think about?

What do I value about this piece? What do I agree or disagree with?

Organization

Form and plot, fluency, and comprehension:

How will I take my readers through my thinking?

What sequence of events or information will make it easy for them to think along with me?

What is the shape of this piece?

How is the author helping me to see it through his or her eyes?

Sentence Fluency

Structure and transitions, vocabulary, and fluency:

Have I included a variety of sentence structures to maintain my reader's interest?

Does one sentence link to another, adding to my overall intent?

Do the sentences help the reader maintain a good pace and one that reflects the shape of the text and my thoughts?

How is the author helping me to link the ideas/information?

Does the piece flow?

How does the author help me read at a good pace?

How do I carry meaning from one part of the text to another?

Voice

Expression, technique, figurative language, rhythm, mood–vocabulary, phonics, phonemic awareness, comprehension:

How do I "bind" the readers to my writing?

How can I control the way they read and the emphasis they get?

What mood do I want to convey?

How do I want them to think and feel?

What tone is inherent? Does it change?

Can I believe everything the author tells me?

What slant is the author presenting?

What am I really thinking and feeling as I read?

Whose thoughts are uppermost–the author's or mine?

Word Choice

Vocabulary, setting–vocabulary, phonics, phonemic awareness, comprehension:

What language will the reader bring?

How can I express my thinking in words that will connect me to my reader?

How will the words I use influence my reader?

How easily can I think about this in my own words?

How does the language help me to understand what the author is telling me?

How do the words help me think more about what I already know?

Conventions

Layout, punctuation, and features–fluency, comprehension:

What will my initial appeal to my reader be?

How will I tell my readers when to pause or to speed up or when to add their own information?

How will I link the illustrations and the text, or the examples and the explanations?

How easy is it for me to give this piece my full attention?

How is the author using punctuation and layout to control the pace and tone of my reading?

On most occasions, a twenty-minute guided writing lesson would not allow sufficient time for a piece to be initiated and taken through to a completed text ready to be shared with the group. This means that some lessons will focus on the planning, others on revision, and so on. However, it is important that students do not see any one section of the process as an isolated part. A skilled reader does not wait until the end of a sentence or paragraph before correcting a miscue. And most skilled writers do not wait until completing a draft of a piece before beginning to revise or edit. The drafting, revising, and editing are interwoven, often wrapped around by prewriting at one end and publishing at the other.

Whatever skill or strategy is emphasized during a guided writing lesson, students should see it as a natural part of writing. If a skill or strategy is taken out of context for explicit instruction and practice, there should be discussion about when and how it is used in the course of "normal" writing. An example where common practice may be at odds with the way a skilled writer operates is the overdose of publishing we sometimes promote. Publishing does not necessarily mean rewriting or being dependent on a computer or displaying a piece of work for any and all to read. Publishing can be any form of sharing or revisiting at the time of writing or later. It can mean reading part or all of a text to a close friend or presenting it orally to a group or class. It can be rewritten in a special book for the author's own enjoyment and reflection.

Following the same pattern in a guided writing session that is used in guided reading will bring security to the students and stability to the management issues that underpin any group work, when the majority of the class is working independently. A similar structure for guided reading and writing will also make it easier to incorporate a guided writing session into a timeslot previously devoted to reading. Readers of this chapter might be thinking "I know guided writing has benefits but I cannot do any more than I am already doing." I believe the economy and depth that can be achieved through linking reading and writing far outweighs any management issues. At the very least, devoting one of the weekly guided reading slots to writing would be a good test for both management considerations but, more importantly, to see the benefits of students being more confident and competent writers and readers. Or each week, two of the daily forty-minute writing blocks could be devoted to guided writing, with the class divided into four groups and two groups meeting with the teacher on each of those days. It is so easy to forget that management is the servant of learning–not the reverse.

PATTERN OF A GUIDED WRITING SESSION

Following the pattern of a guided reading lesson, a guided writing session has three main parts:

■ The introductory section, when discussion, explanations, and demonstrations or examples focus on the new learning through identifying learning targets and success criteria, the vehicle for the new learning, and the students' role

■ The exploration and practice section, when students work individually within the group setting to refine their use of skills and extend their repertoire of techniques and strategies to further their development as confident and competent writers, and when students and the teacher monitor progress toward the learning target

■ The reflection section, when the teacher and students honestly appraise the learning, how it has been achieved, and the degree to which the success criteria have been met and use this to set new individual and group learning goals.

The descriptor "flying solo under supervision" requires active and continuous involvement from the student in all three sections of a lesson.

A guided writing session should begin with students reflecting on the successes and challenges of their learning journey. This could be recalling a moment when a challenge was met, identifying a piece of work (or even a sentence) that brought satisfaction, remembering a complimentary remark from a reader, or identifying progress toward an individual, group, or class target. The same degree of honesty should apply when the difficulties are reviewed. For example:

What part of your writing is proving to be the most challenging?

Are you writing with a fairly even pace, or is it a stop-start bumpy ride?

What is it that is frustrating you as a writer?

Do you think more practice will help you overcome this challenge, or do you need some more guidance?

Are you making progress toward your target?

How will you meet your current challenge?

The Introductory Section Confirms the Students as Writers and Sets Clear Targets for the Session

These questions give the students a clear message that they are responsible for monitoring their progress and thinking about the act of writing as much as what is being written. The teacher can then offer relevant suggestions and confirmation, knowing that these will be relevant and more likely to be accepted than if the lesson began with a flood of ideas that could be taken as restrictions. More importantly, the teacher needs to know the unmet challenges in order to take each student to the brink of the known and, with a gentle nudge, provide sufficient guidance to enable the unknown to become the "new known."

The Students Work Individually within a Supportive Group Setting

A supportive though expectant atmosphere should pervade the exploration and practice section of a lesson. Although the students will be working on their own writing, they should feel confident asking for feedback or help from other group members or the teacher. The instant feedback that the teacher is able to provide in the small-group setting should avoid too many moments of frustration, enabling each student to maintain a steady pace and make progress toward the goal. Continuous observation and monitoring by the teacher can signal appropriate times to intervene for group discussions or give attention to common challenges. However, the majority of time and effort in this section should be one-on-one work between student and teacher, when differentiation of support and feedback nurtures each writer to the "new known." As one target is met, a new one is set to keep learning continuous and successful.

The Most Powerful Feedback Is That Given during the Session

Feedback should be given throughout the lesson the same as in a guided reading lesson, when we do not wait until the end of reading before asking a student to reread a section to avoid miscommunication with the author. Feedback during the writing will avoid the tendency to "mark" surface features before attending to the focus of the lesson. Of course, judicious timing and the nature of the intervention or prompting is crucial. During the prewriting discussion, the teacher can make suggestions or say "Perhaps you could . . ." or "Are you thinking . . .?" All comments are aimed at extending the possibilities for consideration in planning a piece. During the writing, teacher feedback will probably be to cause the student to maintain focus, to provoke re-reading or revision, or to remind the student of the audience for or purpose of the work. When effective feedback is provided during the lesson, the marking that traditionally follows a writing composition should be minimal. Often the work will be of sufficient quality and accuracy that rewriting for sharing (especially if this is an oral presentation) will not be necessary. Students need to know the different purposes and nature of marking and feedback and should be in no doubt that a writer has responsibility in both.

It is essential that a guided session end with some reflection on progress and acknowledgement of effort and new learning, such as:

Students Should be Reflective about the Product and Their Effort

What confidence/expertise did you gain as you wrote that piece?

Look back at your work to consider how much progress you made.

Can you identify a place where you were conscious of applying your new learning?

Think about places where you were conscious of meeting a challenge.

Is there a section of your work that you should signal as a yardstick for future writing?

What would you like me to notice or know about this piece of work?

Emphasizing reflection on the learning rather than only the product leads naturally toward students setting their next personal target and collectively deciding the next step. This does not negate the role of the teacher as the instructor, but firmly places some responsibility on the self-assessing role of the learner.

Supervising in order for "solo flying" to be successful requires the teacher to assume a duck's manner of appearing calm and serene above water, but all the time paddling furiously "behind the scene." And for the student, "solo flying" requires commitment and perseverance or "stickability" in order to give their passengers (readers) a journey they would like to repeat.

PART 4

Caught in the Spell

CHAPTER 7: INDEPENDENT READING
Marsha Riddle Buly

Marsha Riddle Buly has been an educator for over 20 years. Her work has spanned the range from preschoolers through adults, including several working with students in Grades 3 to 8 as a classroom teacher, ESL teacher, and reading specialist and with teachers as a literacy coach, mentor teacher, curriculum coordinator, consultant, and teacher educator. Marsha is currently working as a literacy professor at Western Washington University in Bellingham, Washington, where she helps new and experienced teachers deepen their knowledge related to literacy assessment and instruction. Most recently, Marsha and her husband Phil have been enjoying learning about literacy development in the early years with their preschool daughter, Halina.

CHAPTER 8: INDEPENDENT WRITING
Mary Ann Whitfield

Mary Ann Whitfield has been a teacher for over 25 years. She has been a classroom teacher and a teacher developer, and also a teacher leader for over ten years, working alongside teachers in their classrooms, helping them develop their craft as teachers. She also works as a coordinator for The Learning Network®, training other teacher leaders. Mary Ann seeks learning experiences that challenge her to apply and extend her skills and strategies as a teacher and a teacher developer. Mary Ann lives with her husband Ron in Hutto, Texas.

	Desired Outcome	Student's Activity and Thinking	Support/Guidance	Teacher's Role	Approach
PART 1	Self-awareness	Observing Listening Absorbing *There is something in this for me. I want to be able to do likewise.*	Support	Modeling and inspiring Showing benefits of a skilled reader/ writer in action	Read to or write for
PART 2	Self-correcting	Absorbing and practicing alongside a more knowledge-able other *I want to try to do this. I can practice with someone else.*	Support and guidance	Demonstrating– explicitly explaining– the "how" as well as the "what" to encourage participation	Shared reading/ writing
PART 3	Self-assessing	Practicing and applying in other contexts *I can apply what I have learned as I practice by myself with someone watching and guiding me. I can overcome challenges by thinking about what I am learning. The more I practice, the easier it becomes.*	Guidance	Monitoring through interactive formative assessment (nurturing rather than measuring), questioning, provoking, focusing on how meaning is accessed	Guided reading/ writing
PART 4	Self-improving	Gaining confidence in applying learning and meeting new challenges in self-selected contexts. *I can use what I have learned in other contexts. I can think about ways I can improve. I can use what I have learned to learn new things.*	Guidance and reflection	Observing, assessing through formal formative and perhaps some summative procedures, measuring effectiveness of learning and application Planning next learning target and learning opportunities	Independent reading/ writing

Independent Reading

by Marsha Riddle Buly

CHAPTER 7

P redicting where to find Dawn Christiana in her fourth-grade classroom
during independent reading is always an adventure. Independent
reading isn't just a time to practice reading; it's also a time for Dawn
to get to know her students better as readers and to provide instruction
based on what she knows about each student. In this chapter we focus on
the mode of instruction in which Dawn is engaged, independent reading,
in Grades 3 to 8. Today as we enter the classroom, we see her moving from
student to student to confer, with monitoring clipboard in hand.

WHAT HAPPENS DURING INDEPENDENT READING—AN OVERVIEW

Independent reading is the instructional mode that provides time for readers
to extend practice of skills and strategies acquired as a result of more structured instruction (Mooney 1990). This mode of instruction is just one part of
a carefully designed, structured reading program that must also include modeled and guided reading instruction in addition to monitoring, evaluating,
and goal setting (Fountas and Pinnell 2001; Mooney this volume; Routman
2003).

During this mode of instruction students independently practice reading
skills and strategies while the teacher very intentionally moves from student
to student to provide one-on-one guidance. It's the time when the teacher
and the students are able to see if students are applying what they've been
taught. Independent reading also provides teachers an opportunity to
identify the next teaching points for individual students. The information
gathered from this time with individuals can then be used by the teacher to
guide teaching points during reading conferences and also during guided or
modeled instruction.

In the earlier grades, most students are beginning their journey toward fluent reading. As they begin, they are reading very simple books with minimal storylines and are usually reading these simple stories out loud. A primary classroom is seldom quiet during independent reading. Most students in the upper elementary and middle school grades are well on their way toward fluent and proficient reading and have reading behaviors that enable them to engage independently with rich and meaningful text. In these upper grades, voices may still be heard, but the voices are usually confined to the classroom teacher and a student or small group of students involved in a very intentional teaching and learning conversation with the teacher.

As the teacher roves and confers with students or small groups, he or she observes and makes notes, at all times monitoring for student understanding. The teacher uses a system to ensure that all students receive the conference time, and focus, that each needs and to help the teacher keep track of each student's understandings and next steps about reading.

Most students are quietly practicing skills and strategies in diverse and continually more complex texts. The text, however, must be accessible to each student. This means different texts for different students. And that means that the teacher must be knowledgeable about a wide range of texts and guide the students to appropriate materials. It is in these accessible texts that students in Grades 3 to 8 practice and cement their growing reading skills and strategies. The students often track their own use of reading strategies and respond to what they read in various personal ways. This time to practice is critical, just as it is for any new skill we learn, such as walking, singing, or sports.

ISN'T INDEPENDENT READING JUST SSR, DEAR, OR SQUIRT?

The primary difference between independent reading and times set aside for reading such as Sustained Silent Reading (SSR), Drop Everything and Read (DEAR), or Super Quiet Uninterrupted Reading Time (SQUIRT) is that the material read during independent reading is always at an accessible level to the students and selection of that material is always made or guided by the teacher. Figure 7.1, adapted from several sources (Cunningham and Allington 2003; Fountas and Pinnell 2001; Mooney 1990; Smith and Elley 1997) illustrates key differences between the two.

There should certainly be time within the school day for "free reading," when anything goes, but it should not be confused with the instructional mode of

CAUGHT IN THE SPELL OF WRITING AND READING

Sustained Silent Reading	Independent Reading
Students read self-selected material for a set amount of time	Students read teacher-guided material for a set amount of time
Free choice of materials; students choose	Choice of materials guided by teacher
Teacher spends majority of time modeling voluntary reading or reading at the same time	Teacher spends majority of time monitoring student reading behaviors or providing instruction through one-on-one reading conferences
Student reading time is usually not interrupted	Student reading time is purposefully interrupted for structured teacher conferences
Reports are not necessarily required, although a log of what has been read is often required	A log of reading is kept; strategies and skills taught and learned are tracked
Students are focused on the content of the text	Students may be focused on the content of the text, but the primary focus is on their own use of reading skills and strategies
Material may be at an accessible level	Reading material is at an accessible level
Sharing may occur and is usually focused on the content or ideas from the material read	Sharing may occur and is usually focused on what the reader learned or noticed about him- or herself as a reader

Figure 7.1: Sustained silent reading versus independent reading

reading alone, or independent reading. Independent reading is a carefully structured and intentional instructional approach that must be scheduled into a timeslot as carefully protected as read to, shared reading, guided writing, or math instruction.

As can be seen from the chart in Figure 7.1, sustained silent reading has a different purpose from the instructional mode of independent reading. Unless care is taken, sustained silent reading can result in a waste of valuable student time. I have two main concerns about silent reading time that I suspect are shared by many teachers who have had similar opportunities to spend substantial time in a variety of Grade 3 to 8 classrooms during "sustained silent reading" (SSR). In the hundreds of classrooms that I have visited, I have too often found that the only silent reading time in a day is an unstructured time when students have total free choice over materials; time when the student reads, or looks at, what he or she wants and no monitoring occurs. Often students will pick books because friends were reading the books or because they've seen, or want to see, a movie. The text itself may be far too difficult for the students to successfully engage with the material. Students may "get through it" or be able to say "I read it, but I don't get it," as Cris Tovani (2000) writes about in her book of the same title, but what they have learned or cemented about reading is questionable. Too often students, especially in Grades 6 to 8, are simply hiding behind books that are just too hard for them to read on their own, waiting out the SSR time.

The second main concern I have with sustained silent reading is the use of it as a "time filler." Students get to read when they're done with everything else. There are at least two problems with this. First, it really doesn't provide much incentive for students to read across different genres or even to read. Second, although most teachers believe that there is a correlation between the amount of leisure, or free, reading a child does and reading achievement, Richard Anderson and his colleagues found that on most days the fifth-grade students they studied engaged in little or no book reading (Anderson, Wilson, and Fielding 1988). Long ago, Richard Allington wrote an often discussed article titled "If They Don't Read Much, How They Ever Gonna Get Good?" (1977), in which he presented additional evidence that good readers read more than poor readers. And, according to Barbara Taylor and her colleagues, where that reading occurs is important. Taylor and her colleagues had fifth- and sixth-grade students keep track of the time they spent reading and the location of that reading for about half a year. They found that while the amount of time students spent reading **during** the reading period contributed significantly to higher reading scores; the amount of time students read at home was not significantly related to reading achievement (Taylor, Frye, and Maruyama 1990). It seems evident that if independent reading time is reserved for those who have finished their work in school or left only for home, we can find the Matthew effect (Stanovich 1986); those who are quick at their work and like to read get some time to read, and those who struggle a bit get less time for this important practice. It's too important to be left to chance.

DOES INDEPENDENT READING HELP VOCABULARY GROWTH?

An irrefutable correlation exists between vocabulary and comprehension—and comprehension is what reading should be about! We acquire new vocabulary when we read on our own. The more we read the more vocabulary we encounter and are likely to learn. The more vocabulary we learn, the more words we can easily read, and the greater the possibility that we will understand what we are reading.

Incredibly, by third grade, independent reading can be students' most important vocabulary builder, more so than time spent with basal textbooks or even students' daily oral interactions with peers and adults.

Jim Trelease summarizes research that explains why this is so. First, although oral language is important to developing vocabulary, at older grade levels written language is not the equivalent of oral language written down. Most conversation uses the same 5,000 words, called the Basic Lexicon. We use another 5,000 words less frequently in oral conversation. But the words that really help us to develop our vocabulary and comprehend more are the words beyond these basic 10,000; those words are considered rare. Printed material introduces three to eight times more rare words than conversation does, and it is those rare words that are so critical to reading.

Second, basal readers, especially those with controlled vocabulary, which are making a comeback in the United States, fail to offer readers the same richness of vocabulary, sentence structure, or literary forms that trade books do. Such a lack of rich text is likely to result in students who are not well prepared to read and fully understand the multitude of genres that they will encounter in the world (Trelease 2001).

William Nagy and Richard Anderson claim that good readers may read ten times as many words as poor readers in any given school year (1984). This gives them ten times the opportunity to meet and learn rare words! This combined with the findings of researchers Anderson, Wilson, and Fielding (1988) and Taylor, Frye, and Maruyama (1990), who report data showing that upper elementary and middle school children who spend more time reading show greater gains in reading achievement levels, prove a strong and positive correlation between comprehension and vocabulary.

HOW DOES READING ON OUR OWN STRENGTHEN STRATEGIES AND SKILLS WE'VE ALREADY BEEN TAUGHT?

The National Institute of Child Health and Human Development's National Reading Panel reports that fluent readers can read text with accuracy, speed, and ease so that a text sounds like spoken language when read aloud (2000). This fluent reading demands that readers have well-developed word identification skills, strategies to monitor their understanding, and a wide reading vocabulary. It also demands practice. Consider for a moment any sport or musical instrument that anyone has learned to play successfully. It is not enough to know the rules of the game; the players must have the opportunity to apply the rules in practice.

I often use the example of skiing when I talk to students in Grades 3 to 8 about the different ways we practice and learn and the varying degrees of proficiency we all have with different things. I can get down an expert run–one way or another, while hoping that nobody sees me. I won't call that skiing–just survival with skis. I revert to the most simplistic and basic of strategies I've learned–snowplow, sitting on my bottom, sliding, cursing, and prayer. Clearly, some of these are useful strategies and some aren't, but when frustrated, any strategy pops out–I'm in survival mode! Once down the run, I'm exhausted and ready to quit and get hot chocolate, thankful to have made it to the bottom with no broken bones.

On intermediate runs, it's a different story. I'm at my instructional level. I'm ready to learn new things. I'll watch someone model a move and I'll try it for myself. If I'm lucky, I'll have a teacher or someone who knows more about skiing who can tell me if I'm doing it "right" and guide me in improving the new skiing strategy that I'm trying. I then practice on the intermediate runs, with guidance, but I also practice a lot on the easy runs, where I don't need that guidance.

The easy runs are at my independent level. It's the practice on the easy runs that gives me the fluency and confidence I need to really own the new techniques. On the easy runs I can ski fluently, with grace, and without falling, almost all of the time. I occasionally encounter an unexpected bump or challenge, but I'm able to work through it on my own. It's also the place where it's pretty clear if I haven't learned the strategy–if I can't do it on my own on this simple run, I probably need to be taught again–perhaps shown the strategy in a different way. Similar to a reading conference, I might be shown the strategy on the independent run if an instructor or more knowledgeable other sees that I'm confused about something that I've been taught.

Some of my friends have similar instructional levels. Some are at an instructional level on harder ski runs (even the expert runs) and some have an instructional level on the easier runs. Some of my students have instructional levels for skiing that are higher than mine! The important thing is that I have the opportunity to learn at my instructional level, where the challenges are guided, and to practice at my independent level, where I am able to independently overcome almost any challenge that is presented and where I get lots of time to practice; similar to what occurs during independent reading.

Patricia Cunningham and Richard Allington also suggest providing students with analogies about the importance of practice. They break this into three parts for students and explain that to learn to become good at anything, we need: 1) instruction, 2) practice on the skills, and 3) practice on the whole thing. In reading this means that 1) we need instruction, 2) we need to practice the important skills, and 3) we need to read! They further point out that if we do not make time for students to read in school, we can't expect students to make time to read out of school (Cunningham and Allington 2003, 19). To me, independent reading provides the time for students to practice the important skills that they have been taught in text with minimal challenges, which gives students success, a better chance of engagement, and hopefully the desire to reach for books when they are out of our sight.

WHAT DOES THE NATIONAL READING PANEL SUGGEST ABOUT INDEPENDENT READING?

According to the Report of the National Reading Panel, which considered only experimental studies, there are few published experimental studies related to the development of fluent reading through independent reading (National Institute of Child Health and Human Development 2000). Studies that the National Reading Panel did review were only focused on practices such as sustained silent reading (SSR) rather than on what we're discussing—independent reading. The level of the material that students were reading was not controlled in the experimental studies reviewed. However, a lack of experimental studies doesn't tell us that something isn't good—it tells us that researchers need to keep working on how to study it. It's pretty easy to understand why it's so hard to study the effects of independent or silent reading. How do we control what students read independently outside of the school day? They are surrounded with print–menus, schedules, road signs, brochures, computer programs, shampoo bottles, and cereal boxes–much of it written at an independent level. All of these texts provide opportunities for students to expand their vocabulary and practice their reading skills and strategies. To study independent reading, researchers would probably need to look at the differences in the amount of time children spend reading material that is at their level all day over an extended period of time–a tricky thing to study! In the meantime, we teachers need to do what makes logical sense **and** make sure that we are carefully monitoring the progress of our students. The bottom line is that we need to be intentional about what we do and to make sure that our students are growing as readers. If our assessment and observational data indicate that our students are not growing as readers, then we need to look at, and adjust, the instruction and opportunities that we are providing.

WHAT DOES INDEPENDENT READING LOOK LIKE IN THE SCHOOL DAY?

I started this chapter with a glimpse into Dawn Christiana's classroom. Let's take a closer look. Dawn loops with her students. She meets them as third-grade students, and they stay with her through fourth grade. The literacy block in third and fourth grade looks the same. It begins with a ten-minute demonstration on a reading behavior or key understanding that is needed by all, or the majority of, the students. This is followed by at least a 45-minute time period when students are engaged in reading and responding to text that they have chosen with guidance from Dawn. As students read at their independent level, they pay careful attention to both the content of the material they are reading and to their own reading behaviors. Often this time is longer and combined with independent writing, when students are experimenting with the genres and writing strategies they have been reading. The independent reading time ends with the students coming back together for a brief period of time, no more than five minutes, to share what they have learned about themselves as readers or writers in that day's literacy block. Dawn simply asks her students, "So what did you notice about yourself as readers (or writers) today?"

The heart of the independent reading time is the 45 minutes when students are engaged in text and the intentionality of what Dawn expects her students to be doing. In addition, students know what to expect of Dawn. This is important–the students don't need to watch Dawn and wonder what's next. She has set expectations for what the students are doing as they engage with text. Dawn moves systematically through the classroom, conferring with individual students. For example, if she has been modeling how readers make connections between text and their schema in order to help understand what is read, then the students might be paying special attention to the times when they're reading and they recognize themselves making a connection. Dawn might ask students to simply put a self-stick note or marker on a page when they notice a connection. Then, after reading, students are asked to return to the page and think about the connection and how it was helpful, or not, to them as readers.

The following examples show different ways that Dawn, and another teacher, Kim Gasper, guide students' metacognition during independent reading time while at the same time providing the teachers information about their students' understandings.

In this first example, the class has been working on recognizing how connections help readers better understand text. Mary recognized that she had made a text-to-self connection with *The Name Jar* (Choi 2001) because she had experience moving to a new school, where no one knew her name. Mary recognized that the story was better for her because she could relate to it. Mary's response demonstrates her understanding.

Example 1: Recognizing How Connections Help Readers Better Understand Text

In this second example, Joseph realized that he had visualized when he was reading *The Mystery of Ben Franklin's Ghost* (Cosson 1999). He completed a Visualizing Double Entry Journal (see Figure 7.2) that Dawn had modeled during a previous whole class mini-lesson. Joseph described the author's description and how, as a result, he could visualize all the kids in front of the house just standing there. When Joseph first filled out the form, he had not added the last sentence. Dawn recognized a teaching point for Joseph. Joseph wasn't thinking about, or at least was not documenting his thinking about, how the author's words had led him to the visualization. After Dawn's brief but intentional mini-lesson reading conference on this teaching point with Joseph, he added the last sentence.

Example 2: Visualizing While Reading

The third example came toward the end of the year in Kim's fifth-grade class. Inferring is a hard strategy to both teach effectively and for students to demonstrate at any age. Bobby had been reading *Jin Woo* (Bunting 2001). As he read, he knew he was to track his thinking with self-stick notes. To do this, he was to write a question, and then as he read, Bobby was to write the text that helped him to answer his question. He was also to write how he used his schema to make an inference from the text. This

Example 3: Demonstrating a Need for More Support about Inference

Visualizing Double Entry Journal

I make pictures in my mind from what I read...these pictures help me understand the story better!

When I was reading The Mystery of Ben Franklin's ghost. The author was telling me that there where a lot of kid but no were to play. And there wasn't a park for a few miles and the kids were on the street. In sted of the old park there was a gass stashon and market. I could just Vivualiz all the kids infrot of the house just standing there.

Figure 7.2: Joseph's visualizing double entry journal

was all modeled and guided previously during other modes of instruction. Following reading, Bobby was to take the self-stick notes and apply each to a form that Kim had modeled during a demonstration. Bobby was then to explain the inference he had made from the text and his schema. Kim checks both the understanding that the students get from the independent book read and assesses their understanding of the strategy that she focuses on during the more supportive modes of modeled and guided reading. The fact that Bobby, and most of his classmates, struggled to get even one inference on paper suggested to Kim that she needed to move back to a more supportive mode of instruction and continue to model and guide inferring.

Dawn also has students periodically self-evaluate their independent reading. Dora gave herself a score of "3" on the self-evaluation. Dora wrote, "I read most of the time. I read books at my level and more than my level. And I always know my interests. And I always read my interests." José's justification for a score of 4 was, "Once I get started on a book I can't stop reading. I can read any book I'm assigned to do. Reading is my favorite activity to do in school. I like finishing my books fast, because I have other books waiting for me to read."

In some classrooms, a rubric like the one that Dawn uses for self-evaluation of independent reading is used each day. As students finish reading, they self-evaluate and give themselves a score. Sometimes teachers will have students add a reflection on what they need to do the next day to make independent reading even more effective for them–such as "get started immediately, have a book ready, check my understanding." Once modeled, the self-evaluation can be as simple as an addition to a reading log. The reading log provides a means for both students and teachers to keep track of the types of books read, the length of time it is taking to get through books, and the students' self-evaluation. After students note the date, the book read, and pages read, a column is added for a self-evaluation score, similar to the example in Figure 7.3.

Example 4: Using Self-Evaluation

Date	Title	Pages Read	Self-evaluation
5/13	Jin Woo	15–45	3–focused, started on time

Figure 7.3: A form for student self-evaluation

5 minutes	Settling in, teacher reads along with students
35 minutes	All students reading, teacher roves, one-on-one conferences, observational notes, monitoring notes, oral reading records Teacher can systematically meet with between 3 and 5 students each day
5 minutes	Meeting together—students or teacher sharing, reflections about strategy use during reading, book talks or recommendations, self-evaluations, changing books, record keeping

Figure 7.4: A sample independent reading block for Grades 3 to 8

Some teachers prefer to have an isolated independent reading time that follows a demonstration. The table in Figure 7.4 provides an example of one way to structure an independent reading block in Grades 3 to 8. Note that as the students settle into their books, the teacher briefly engages in reading. There is value in a classroom teacher briefly modeling his or her joy at getting lost in a book. Some students rarely have a chance to see adults reading books for pleasure. In addition, the texts that the teacher reads act as material for the teacher to provide real examples of strategy use and reading behaviors. The teacher can use his or her own book to model for the students in the next day's mini-lesson. But beware—it's easy to get lost in a book! Primarily because of the overly full school day, this modeling must be brief, using no more than five minutes of this rich instructional independent reading time. Then the teacher uses the remainder of the time to observe and confer with students. Individualized instruction takes place during these conferences.

THE READING CONFERENCE

The key to successful independent reading is in the reading conference. This one-on-one instructional moment often provides the most effective opportunity to teach someone a strategy or understanding they are ready to use. Let's peek into Becky Smith's eighth-grade classroom as she confers with James.

Becky moves a chair next to James and asks, "How's it going?" James knows that this will be the opening question in the reading conference. He doesn't seem surprised, and in fact seems prepared to answer. He puts a marker in his book because he knows that Becky will want him to read a little of it to her, and he begins to converse with Becky as she proceeds through a set of familiar questions to James—there are no surprises from the teacher. This

CAUGHT IN THE SPELL OF WRITING AND READING

predictable structure is crucial to a successful reading conference. Both teacher and student need to know what to expect during the conference. This allows students to focus on what they are doing without wondering what the teacher is going to do. It also allows the student to be prepared for the conference, which helps keep the conference short and to the point. The key is that the students are taught about the structure and conferences are modeled before they take place in a class.

Becky asks the following questions:

1. What are you reading? (or "How is it going" if this is a book that the student was reading during the last conference)

2. What's the most interesting thing that's happened or that you've read? Why?

3. What's been happening or what have you learned or read about so far?

4. What are your thoughts or reactions to this book/text so far?

5. What do you think will happen next or what do you think you'll find out next? Why?

6. Is there anything you need my help with?

7. Would you read the next "two pages" (about 200 words) to me?

8. Tell me what you remember about what you just read.

9. Was there a part that was confusing or that didn't make sense to you either in what you just read or in another part of the book?

Becky wants to start the conference with a focus on the meaning of what is being read. This is, after all, the ultimate goal of reading. At the same time, Becky wants to move the conference to each student's reading behaviors. Is the student predicting? Inferring? Questioning? Monitoring for understanding?

If a student tells Becky he has finished reading, then Becky starts with the following:

1. Did you enjoy this book/text? Why?

2. Would you read this book/text again? Why?

3. Is this a book/text you would recommend to others? Why?

4. Have you read other books by the same author?

5. How do these books compare to this book, or how does a TV or movie version compare to this text?

6. Was there any place you noticed that you (used a fix-up strategy, got stuck, and so on)? What did you do?

7. Ask the student to read about 200 words from any part of the text to get a feel for how the reading went.

8. What are you going to read next?

As the student is reading, Becky takes a modified record of oral reading. She notes the name of the book and pages read, then notes miscues and observations about strategy use and miscues. Becky notes any patterns that she observes. If the book is too hard, she can then help the student to consider the text choice. Listening to just about 200 words allows Becky an opportunity to quickly monitor for fluency, appropriate rate, accuracy, and fix-up strategies and to keep track of changes over time through her notes. Becky will then do one of the following: reinforce a strategy previously taught in a conference, guided, or whole group setting; teach a new strategy based on either the student's questions or Becky's monitoring; or move to the next student. Becky does assess with more formal assessments at other times. She has tried both the Development Reading Assessment grades 4–8 (Beaver and Carter 2004) and the Qualitative Reading Inventory 3 (Leslie and Caldwell 2001) but doesn't use these rather lengthy assessments during the reading conference. The reading conference time is used to meet with many students for a brief period of time. When Becky decides that she needs more information in order to be more intentional and accurate in her teaching points for a student, she might use a planning time or a different part of the day to conduct a lengthier assessment.

Some questions that Becky might ask following the oral reading, depending on her purpose with a particular student, are:

■ What are you doing well in reading?

■ What are you working on/want to work on right now?

■ What are you learning about yourself as a reader through this reading? How is it helping you work on your goals?

■ What are you going to read next? (The answer to this question helps Becky guide the student to a book at his level that will be of interest).

Kim Gasper, who teaches a combination of fifth and sixth grade, has incorporated many of these questions and other useful conference tracking devices into a friendly format (Figure 7.5). Kim's reading conference sheet was inspired by the strategies from *Mosaic of Thought* (Keene and Zimmermann 1997), *Strategies*

Student: **Tomas**

Date: **5/13/05**

Title: **The Hoopster by Alan Lawrence**

Picture Book (Chapter Book) Comic Book
Magazine Non-Fiction Other

BOOK CHOICE
- Why did you pick this book? Title/Cover Pictures Genre Series (Subject Matter) Author Friend/Parent/Teacher (Recommendation) Blurb Other

  Mom bought bc I like basketball

- Is this book easy, just right or challenging for you? How do you know? Easy (Just Right) Challenging ___218___ pages

  some big words like "congratulations"

RETELL
- What page are you on? **144** Tell me what this is about and what's been going on so far. (Theme)
  (Setting) (Characters) (Main Events/Key Ideas) (Details) Problem Solution Dialogue Text Supported Teacher Prompts 4 3 2 1

  *Kid likes basketball, lived of time of racism. Andrey's black friend Sean white
  job - wrote article, boss liked
  cousin - Cedric*

OPINION
- What do you think of the story/text? Why do you think that?

  I like it bc it's interesting. Not just all about basketball. Other issues, fighting

STRATEGY DISCUSSION →

READ ALOUD/RUNNING RECORD
- Read this part aloud for me.
  Tell me what you remember about what you just read.
  Was there a part that was confusing or didn't make sense?

  *Boss reading all letters he got about article what
  + people liked about article
  Boss promoted him. — — —*

TRICKY WORDS
- Any tricky words for you? (or words from oral reading)
  (Sound out) Clues Word Knowledge Pictures TP (Gave) No errors

  *P.144 compassionate   article   ✓ disillusioned
  straightforward
  articulate (Gave) ← bravura
  contributing*

PREDICTION
- What do you think will happen? What makes you think that?
  Random (Reasonable) (Text Supported) Inference

  *He'll tell isdad about promotion dad
  will be proud bc dad dropped out of college. Andrey only family in col.*

STRATEGY DISCUSSION
Schema/Connections 4 3 2 1
Questioning 4 3 2 1   *sister doing drugs, why? in book - all friends doing it maybe forced, that's cool "peer pressure"*
Visualizing 4 3 2 1
Inferring 4 3 2 1
Determining Importance 4 3 2 1
Summarizing 4 3 2 1
Synthesizing 4 3 2 1
Monitoring Comprehension/Fix-up Strategies 4 3 2 1

STRENGTHS	GOALS	TEACHING POINTS / NEXT STEPS
What are you doing well in reading? WS. - quiet break apart words to sound out	What are you working on / want to work on right now? *more fluently . RAH 15-20* Goal 25 mins 4x/wk What are you learning about yourself as a reader through this reading? How is it helping you work on your goals? *I don't know. Maybe some big words - sound out*	• take more specific notes on wj. - quote text • reflect on reader • main/determining what's important
Teacher Observations:	How long do you think it will take you to finish this book/text? *by next* What do you think you want to read next? *How to Eat Fried Worms*	

Figure 7.5: Sample conference and tracking questions for the middle grades
Form © 2006 by Kim Gasper

that Work (Harvey and Goudvis 2000), *Reading Essentials* (Routman 2003), and a Reading Conference Rubric found on The Reading Lady website.

In the example of Tomas's conference, Kim found out that Tomas was self-selecting chapter books that were at his level. She was able to observe Tomas making connections between the world and his own life and also to observe that Tomas was asking questions about what was happening. Tomas was able to tell Kim about what he was doing well as a reader (visualizing) and to set goals for himself. Teachers that Kim has shared this form with have also found it useful and easy. In fact, Kim's student teacher wanted to be sure that I was going to include the form in this chapter. The first conference that the student teacher did took a little longer as he became familiar with the format. But after the first experience, conferences took less than five minutes with each student.

Dawn also has a format that she uses to help her with reading conferences. The format changes throughout the year as Dawn focuses on different areas. In the example from the beginning of the year of Limny's conference (Figure 7.6), the format is quite simple. Three things happen during the conference. First, Dawn asks, "What have you learned about yourself as a reader?" Second, Dawn asks the student to read to her as she takes a record of oral reading. Third, Dawn and the student set personal next steps for him or her as a reader. The format that Dawn uses allows her to document four conferences on one sheet of paper, providing a quick way for Dawn to refer back to what has come before. Later in the year Dawn modified the reading conference form (Figure 7.7), shown here reflecting Chloe's use of strategies that have been teaching points throughout the year.

MONITORING STUDENT PROGRESS OUTSIDE THE READING CONFERENCE

Independent reading time also provides opportunities for monitoring student progress outside of the one-on-one conference. Teachers can be making systematic observations and either teacher or student can be keeping track of student behaviors such as the following, adapted from *Reading for Life* (Ministry of Education 1997) and *Reading in Junior Classes* (Ministry of Education 1985):

■ What books students are reading

■ How long students are spending on a book

■ What strategies and sources of information students use to solve meaning and word difficulties

Reading conference notes:

Limny

Reflect, Data, Goal

1. What have you learned about yourself as a reader?
2. Read to me, discuss, share
3. Personal next steps as a reader

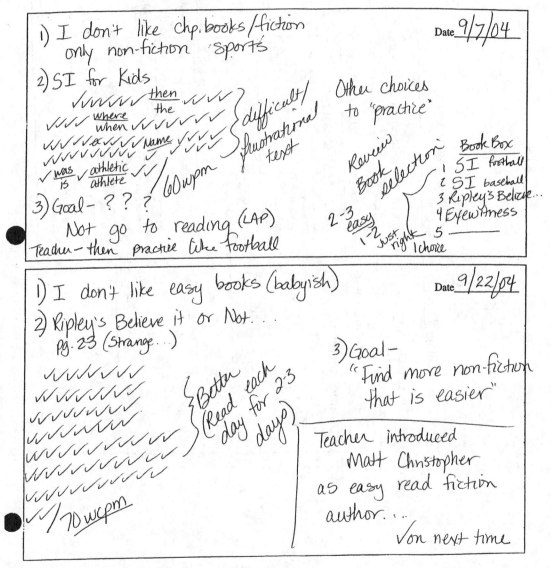

Figure 7.6: Simple conference format for beginning of the school year
Form © 2006 by Dawn Christiana

Name: Chloe   **Date:** 2/11/05

Reading Conference

What I am reading: Lemony Snicket #1

What have you learned about yourself as a reader through this reading? I like fantasy and this book is easier than last book (Tale of Despereaux)

What are your current reading goals? Series... Read even more (longer time in school 😊)

Running Record:	Strategy Discussion:				Strengths:
		superior	proficient	emerging	not present
silent	**Connections:** Comment: Like the movie - Also Harry Potter...		✓	—	—	Attitude improve! yes
136 words	**Questioning:** Comment: I wonder if...	—	✓	—	—	Variety of text
✓✓✓✓✓✓✓✓ ✓✓✓✓✓✓ ✓✓✓	**Visualizing:** Comment: (still literal - not "movie"/show)	—	—	✓	—	Fluency & s/expression
Great expression!	**Inferring:** Comment:	—	—	—	✓	
128 words	**Determining Importance** Comment:	—	—	✓	—	**Areas for growth:** (Teaching points)
	Summarizing: Comment: Then then then... (goal)	—	—	✓	—	- Summarize (not all...)
Fix-Up Strategies: repeat, pause	**Synthesizing:** Comment:	—	—	—	✓	- Depth of comp. (strat.)

Figure 7.7: Revised conference format for later in the school year
Form © 2006 by Dawn Christiana

- Other times that students read

- Who the students talk or write to about books

- How the students know they have made a good choice

- How students choose books

- What students do when they are reading a book that is too hard

- Who students' favorite authors are

- Whether students consistently choose books that present too many difficulties or restrict their choices to books that present few or no challenges

- If students becomes absorbed in text or simply flip pages

- If students understand and make use of text features such as illustrations, captions, the table of contents, and so on

- If students seek help immediately when meeting a challenge or try to overcome challenges independently.

Teacher monitoring of student understanding takes place in a number of ways. Kim likes to use labels (Figure 7.8), as illustrated on Alex's and Tatiana's conference forms. Kim takes notes on labels during independent reading, during guided reading groups, and as she is monitoring or observing the room. She differentiates, on the label, the situation where she has made an observation (IR = independent reading, GR = guided reading, M = monitoring class). Kim then transfers the labels to a notebook with sections for each student and considers the teaching point for the student based on her notes and observations.

Becky prefers a class chart (Figure 7.9) because she is able to see at a glance which students need conferences and who has similar needs (information that she can then use to form guided reading groups). For some teachers this system works wonderfully. For others, starting with a notebook is more manageable.

A small looseleaf notebook with a tab for each student has worked well for me. The front of the notebook contains copies of the student meeting schedule. I keep multiple copies and date when I have met with students so that I, or anyone else, can tell what day of the cycle we are in. Following that, I keep

Student: _____ Tatiana

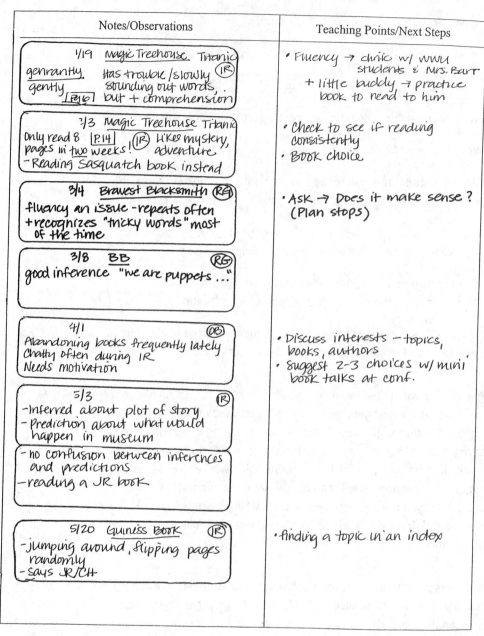

Notes/Observations	Teaching Points/Next Steps
1/19 Magic Treehouse. Titanic genrantly Has trouble/slowly (IR) gently sounding out words, [P.16] but + comprehension	• Fluency → clinic w/ WWU students & Mrs. Bart + little buddy → practice book to read to him
2/3 Magic Treehouse Titanic Only read 8 [P.14] (IR) Likes mystery, pages in two weeks! adventure - Reading Sasquatch book instead	• Check to see if reading consistently • Book choice
3/4 Bravest Blacksmith (RG) fluency an issue - repeats often + recognizes "tricky words" most of the time	• Ask → Does it make sense? (Plan stops)
3/8 BB (RG) good inference "we are puppets..."	
4/1 (DB) Abandoning books frequently lately Chatty often during IR Needs motivation	• Discuss interests - topics, books, authors • Suggest 2-3 choices w/ mini book talks at conf.
5/3 (IR) - Inferred about plot of story - Prediction about what would happen in museum - no confusion between inferences and predictions - reading a JR book	
5/20 Guiness Book (IR) - jumping around, flipping pages randomly - says JR/CH	• finding a topic in an index

Figure 7.8: Examples of teacher's monitoring notes on labels
Form © 2006 by Kim Gasper

DATA Collection Chart

Student: _____	Student: _____	Student: _____
Strengths:	Strengths:	Strengths:
Areas for Improvement:	Areas for Improvement:	Areas for Improvement:
Student: _____	Student: _____	Student: _____
Strengths:	Strengths:	Strengths:
Areas for Improvement:	Areas for Improvement:	Areas for Improvement:
Student: _____	Student: _____	Student: _____
Strengths:	Strengths:	Strengths:
Areas for Improvement:	Areas for Improvement:	Areas for Improvement:
Student: _____	Student: _____	Student: _____
Strengths:	Strengths:	Strengths:
Areas for Improvement:	Areas for Improvement:	Areas for Improvement:

Figure 7.9: A class chart focusing on the needs of the student
Form © 2006 by Kim Gasper as adapted from Dawn Christiana

a chart of modeled class lessons. Then, behind each student's tab there are several pages for monitoring notes, oral reading records, and an ongoing list of individual conference topics. This notebook must never be lost! It is my plan book and my grade book for this part of my instructional reading program.

The examples described earlier that Dawn used to guide metacognition provide evidence of learning outside of the conference. Reading response letters provide another example. Jacob wrote to Dawn about a dinosaur book he had read (Figure 7.10). Because the words were easy for him to navigate he was able to focus on critical reading of the book. He noticed that even though the book had a copyright of 1997 much of the information was no longer accurate, and he provided examples of his findings. He also provided Dawn with his version of a phonetic pronunciation of the names of dinosaurs because he knew that Dawn would want to be able to pronounce the names. His letter provides Dawn with a means to see how well he has understood his reading and the thinking he was doing as he read. Her response allows her to guide him to think about the author's use of captions.

SYSTEMS

It is critical to meet with all students on a regular basis. That doesn't necessarily mean meeting with all students for the same amount of time, but it does mean a regular check in. For example, if in a class period with 27 students I have five students who I know have greater needs in the area of reading, I'm going to meet with them more frequently, but not to the exclusion of the more proficient readers.

An example of one way to structure regular time with all students appears in Figure 7.11. Assuming that the teacher has an independent reading block at least four days of the week, the teacher will have met with each student at least once in two weeks, and with struggling readers at least twice, as shown by the asterisks. I write "at least once" because when the teacher has the structure down, it may be possible to conduct more than four conferences on a given day. Using this structure, the classroom teacher needs only to know what day of the rotation it is.

KNOWING WHAT TO TEACH

You now have a system in place to make sure you meet with each student. Your students are all engaged in reading at their independent level and have had a role in the choice of material, which means there is a good chance that they're actually reading. The students are managing themselves and

Dear Mrs C.

I like the book Dinosaurs.
Its a flip book that shows all
the dinosaurs but a qustoin I have
is for a book made in 1997
it so out of date...and I noticed
a lot of books are titled dinosaurs
so wouldent it be confuzing for the
libary to find that book on the
computer? I bet you don't saur
means. It means liserd. Many people
think that when you say dinosaur
they picture a large meat eater. But
relly dinosaurs came in all sorts of
sizes. Take cosagnathus (kon-sug-na-thus)
the smallest dinosaur. He was smaller
than a chiken. On Diodoaus (diado,cus)
Was the size of one and a half
of a tennes corts. Im botherd that

Figure 7.10: A response-to-reading letter between student and teacher

the illastrater drew the backround like it is. Why? Because the backround is a lot diffrent then it sould be. I mean Bareonecke lived in a forest not a desert! The book was OK.
Your frend
'Jacob

Dear Jacob,   11/23/04
    I am so excited that you are becoming a "critical" reader. That means you are using what you know in your head and from other books to decide if this non-fiction book is accurate. Did the illustrations have captions to explain why the illustrator might have drawn the setting so differently? I agree that there seem to be a lot of books

Figure 7.10: (Continued)

with the title Dinosaur, but maybe they use other information to sort library books? I'd be interested to so how the information in your 1997 book compared to a 2003 or 2004 book because scientists are learning new things all the time. I am actually thinking of a book Nathaniel and I read together called Dinosaur Sue. They just discovered her bones in Montana—that's after 1997—so the paleontologists know more now.

Keep up the critical reading!

Mrs. C

Figure 7.10: *(Continued)*

Independent Reading Block # → Student ↓	1	2	3	4	5	6	7	8
1. Alice		X						
2. Bob		X						
3. Maria		X						
4. *Antonio	X		X					
5. Isai			X					
6. *Katie	X			X				
7. Alejandro			X					
8. Igor			X					
9. Dasia				X				
10. *Vataliy	X			X				
11. Evan				X				
12. Linda D.					X			
13. *LeAnne	X				X			
14. Courtney					X			
15. Kimberly					X			
16. Amanda						X		
17. Linda C.						X		
18. *Chase		X				X		
19. Evan						X		
20. Phil							X	
21. Rosemary							X	
22. Tracy							X	
23. David							X	
23. Bruce								X
25. Rochelle								X
26. Carmen								X
27. Eugenia								X

Figure 7.11: A table for tracking conferences during independent reading time
Form © 2006 by Marsha Riddle Buly

CAUGHT IN THE SPELL OF WRITING AND READING

they're keeping track of their reading. You've committed to giving reading conferences a try, but you're worried–and your worry is one shared by many teachers getting started with one-on-one conferences. In my experience the biggest hurdle to reading conferences has to do with teachers worrying about knowing what to teach or say in the individual conference and about whether the teacher has selected the "right" teaching point to discuss with a student. There isn't one right lesson for any student or one right set of conference questions. There are undoubtedly several teaching points that would be useful to any student at a given time. The key is to focus on one teaching point at a time and to let the student's reading and the conversation guide your focus.

Usually the focus in a conference during independent reading time is on something that has already been taught during either modeled or guided reading. I keep a list of the strategies that I've modeled. Sometimes I have students keep a list in their reading log of what I have modeled or reinforced. I can then easily refer the student back to the strategy that we've discussed, perhaps by saying, "Remember when we talked about inferring when we were reading poetry last week? We talked about why we infer and how . . . (remind the student of the specific strategy you wish to highlight). I think that trying that with this book is going to help you understand this text better. Let's try it together . . ."

Dawn keeps charts in her room of the strategies that have been modeled. The charts are reminders of what the strategy is, why it's important, and what it looks like when it is being used. The charts are usually created with students or by students. Dawn can easily refer students or groups of students to the strategy during a reading conference or during a small group conference.

The last but most important point about choosing what to teach is to trust what you know about reading. Trust what you know about the student. When you are wondering about what to teach, start by asking yourself questions such as these:

- What do I do as a reader in this situation?

- What else could I do?

- Would this help the student I'm conferring with?

Read more about areas in which you feel less confident. Talk with your colleagues. Check your district or state expectations to give you ideas of what skills the students are expected to be able to use on their own. Then

Teacher Responsibility	Student Responsibility
■ Allow for independent practice of learned strategies ■ Guide and monitor book selection ■ Provide information about a range of sources of text–how to choose text at an accessible level and how to find texts ■ Introduce and have available multiple samples at a range of levels for all genres introduced in class ■ Keep a large classroom library in addition to access to the school library ■ Monitor reading behaviors on a regular basis.	■ Use opportunities to practice what is already known, refine and consolidate what they are learning, and attempt what they are just discovering ■ Play an active role in text selection and monitoring difficulty of text chosen ■ Assume responsibility for reading at independent level ■ Overcome challenges independently ■ Seek regular feedback ■ Use reading for a variety of purposes ■ Participate in teacher-student conferences.

Figure 7.12: Teacher and student responsibilities for independent reading

consider whether the individual student on whom you are focusing is ready for a particular strategy or skill, or if there is something else the student needs to learn first in order to be ready. Think back to those first days of standing in front of the classroom and recognize that your confidence will come and your students will benefit from the instruction you provide. You will find the format, the questions, and your own system for making sure that you are teaching the strategies that will benefit each student.

TEACHER AND STUDENT RESPONSIBILITIES

During independent reading the teacher and students both have responsibilities. The table in Figure 7.12 outlines some of the major areas for each (adapted from Fountas and Pinnell 2001).

GUIDING STUDENTS TO TEXT

Marcella Hu Hsueh-Chao and Paul Nation report that for a text to be helpful to a reader in acquiring new vocabulary, the text needs to be about 98% comprehensible (2000). That's exactly the comprehensibility we want to see in the texts we choose for independent reading. The material needs to have few challenges and readers need to be able to overcome any challenge independently during this mode of instruction. The match between student and text is crucial to engagement and successful learning.

For early readers, the teacher makes the match between reader and text, but as readers develop, especially in third grade and beyond, students need to learn how to select appropriate text both for their own purposes and for purposes supplied by teachers. For example, if a current unit of study in a classroom is technical reading, the classroom teacher must be sure to have a wide range of materials—not just books—from this genre available so that students can independently, as well as instructionally, apply what they are learning about the genre. Simple levels alone are not enough. The teacher needs to have selected books in the genre in which students will be interested, can be offered choice, and in which students can achieve independent success. There also needs to be an expectation in the class that the students will read in this genre. This includes skillfully interesting students in genres with which they might not have yet engaged and artfully helping students to understand the connections between these genres and real life. Building this interest, curiosity about, and understanding of other genres occurs primarily during the modes of modeled and guided instruction in reading and writing, but all are reinforced during reading conferences. This then can lead to unforced choice of topics within accessible levels for practice during independent reading. Choice is important, even during the instructional mode dedicated to independent reading. But choice does not necessarily mean free to choose anything. It is the teacher's responsibility to provide choice that will both interest and stretch students as readers.

We need to help students to engage in independent reading of materials that will further their learning and stretch their thinking without frustrating them. This is especially crucial because adolescents entering the world today will do more reading and writing tasks than at any other time in human history. Yet what that reading and writing looks like will be very different from what it looked like 25 or 50 years ago. The range of materials that people must be able to navigate has become incredibly more complex as technology has developed. This is one main reason that total free choice of reading materials is not what our students need. Guiding material choice gives teachers the opportunity to help students make the connection between reading in school and reading out of school, when the life-long habit of being a reader is reinforced.

In Grades 3 to 8, texts often have many words on a page. The goal for independent reading is that the student can recognize at least 95% of the words with ease. I find that a helpful tool for students is the five-finger rule. Open a book to the middle. Start to read a page. Each time you come to a word that you don't know and can't figure out, put up one finger. If you end up with all five fingers opened on one hand before you get to the end of the page, then this is probably a better book to read at a different time or later in the year. I also find it helpful for students to have at least two books ready to go at any time so that if they lose interest in one or finish one, they're ready to go with another. The expectation must be that during independent reading students are actively engaged with reading or responding to text that is pretty easy for them to read on their own.

Jacob's reading response letter about dinosaurs, described earlier (Figure 7.10) provides a vivid example of what can happen when students read books they are interested in and that are at their independent level. Jacob was a very proficient reader. In the fourth grade many would say he had a reading level well into middle school. Two weeks before he read the dinosaur book he had chosen a picture book, *Halloween* (Seinfeld 2002). The book was at his independent level; it was easy for him to read. He chose it because he recognized the author's name, had an interest in the topic (comedy), and knew it was a book that he could easily read. As a result, he was able to think deeply about the content–demonstrating his connections to the story, as you can read in his letter to Dawn in Figure 7.13.

In Becky's eighth-grade classroom students evaluate how they did as readers each day on a scale of 1 to 4. A score of 4 includes the following criteria: Chose a book that I could read, started to read as soon as it was time, stayed with the text, and monitored my reading. She also has students keep track of the books they are reading in a log and requires a certain number of books to be read in the genre of focus each reporting period. Kim has similar expectations in her fifth-grade classroom.

LAST REMINDERS

The inconclusive results of the report of the National Reading Panel (National Institute of Child Health and Human Development 2000) have been misinterpreted in schools in many ways regarding independent reading. Independent reading appears to be critical to our development as skilled readers, growth in vocabulary, understanding of genres, comprehension, and self-confidence. Through this mode of instruction, we hope that we will help develop children who have practiced and deeply learned the skills and strategies they need to be successful in a variety of text forms and genres and that they choose to

Dear Mrs C.

I love the story Halloween by Jerry Seinfeld. Its funny and yet so true. I mean donts you think a did would want all that candy. Or that the mask would always break and you wouldnt be able to see or breathe or walk. I love the illustrations because it looks so real and it seems like James Bennett drew it before Seinfeld wrote it. I like Jerry Seinfeld because he makes it sound like its in real life. I like Seinfeld because hes a comedian. Sort of like me. He has a stage and used to have his own show which is called Seinfeld. I like the book Halloween.

Your frend

Jacob

Figure 7.13: Jacob's reading response letter about a picture book

become life-long readers. There is enough evidence to say **don't** stop independent reading in your Grades 3 to 8 classrooms and to be intentional about what happens. Guide students as they choose books, scaffold the independent responses from students, include purposeful reading conferences, and hold your students accountable for this instructional time. As students engage in the instructional mode of independent reading, you will find the time you need to focus on individual readers while knowing that students you are not directly next to are matched with appropriate text and practicing the strategies that should help them to become successful life-long readers. It's an important, and valid, use of classroom time!

Independent Writing
by Mary Ann Whitfield

CHAPTER 8

Independent writing is an approach that provides students the opportunity to practice in their own pieces of writing the skills and strategies that they are learning. It is a time for the learners to fly solo, applying their new learning by integrating it with what they are already able to do as writers. Independent writing occurs as learners develop "competence and confidence to be able to choose their own topics, problem-solve, and monitor and set goals themselves with minimum assistance" (Routman 2005, 72). The goal of independent writing is to develop self-improving writers—writers who can apply and extend what they have learned in new contexts and in new ways. Students learn to think, "I can try to use what I have learned in other places—I can think about ways I can improve—I can use what I have learned to learn new things" (Mooney 2005, 26). Students internalize what they are learning and transfer their understandings and skills to new areas, assuming responsibility to problem-solve independently as they plan, draft, revise, proofread, and share their writing.

To become self-improving writers, students take responsibility for setting goals, evaluating their progress toward those goals, and planning for their own next steps. As they self-evaluate, students ask themselves:

- What am I learning to do as a writer?

- What are my strengths?

- What are my goals for improvement?

- How do I plan to achieve my goals?

As students plan how they will achieve their goals they determine what they can do for themselves and what they need help to learn. Help may come in the form of feedback from peers or their teacher. It may also come from analyzing what other writers do and applying it to their own writing. Students

---

CHAPTER 8 INDEPENDENT WRITING

consider when and how they will seek feedback and use models of good writing as they work toward their own learning goals.

Because students are assuming the responsibility for their learning, as they write independently, the teacher is able to assess what learning has been acquired and determine how the students are now able to apply that learning. The teacher carefully monitors students' independent writing and uses that information to plan for future instruction.

DEVELOPING INDEPENDENCE IN WRITERS

Independence is the goal for students and does not come as an endpoint in the learning sequence, but rather is gained through regular practice (Mooney 1990; 2005). The teacher provides many opportunities for students to attain the goal of independence by including independent writing in the daily schedule of the classroom along with the other instructional approaches of writing. Independent writing experiences offer opportunities for students to write for their own purposes, selecting their own topics, audiences, and appropriate forms in addition to writing on assigned topics and/or forms.

Time to practice writing is crucial to the development of the writer. "Just as it is necessary to do a great deal of independent reading to become a competent reader, so too is it with writing" (Routman 2005, 72). As students write independently, they develop their ideas, making decisions about what they want to say and how they will say it. Students experience the power of expressing their thoughts through written and visual language for different purposes in a variety of forms. They also face the struggles and challenges that writers encounter as they work to develop and articulate their ideas. These times of struggle and challenge are a necessary part of developing independence, causing the learners to become more conscious of the understandings they have as writers and how they can use those understandings to express themselves in writing. As students become more aware of their understandings, they learn how to apply their skills in new ways and to extend their skillfulness.

During independent writing, the teacher avoids interrupting the thinking and actions of the students as much as possible so that the student writers can make independent decisions and take responsibility for creating their own meaning. This time for independent problem-solving gives students a strong sense of ownership not just of the text they are currently creating but also of the process of writing. Because students are writing by themselves, the teacher is able to assess the skills and understandings each learner has taken to independence and to recognize the learning that still needs to be supported.

INDEPENDENT WRITING IN GRADE 3 AND UP

While there are similarities to independent writing in kindergarten through Grade 2, independent writing in Grade 3 and up presents students with even greater opportunities to transfer and apply what they have learned to new areas and in new ways as they are expected to use writing as a tool for learning in all the content areas. Students in higher grades are able to use the understandings and skills developed from their early writing experiences more automatically and fluently. As students move through upper elementary and middle school, they must learn to sustain writing for longer periods of time. The teacher ensures that there is adequate time in the daily and weekly schedule for independent writing. Students are now ready to practice on a deeper level the skills of analyzing, critiquing, and evaluating their own writing and the writing of others. In the early grades students begin to use writing as a tool for learning, and in Grade 3 and up students become more independent in the use of this tool and extend its application. Students need encouragement and opportunities to use writing for problem solving in all content areas, both with support and independently. These problem-solving experiences develop understandings of concepts, knowledge, and skills in content areas, such as math, science, and social studies, in addition to the language arts.

Independent writing is essential in the development of the characteristics of a proficient writer. Figure 8.1 compares the characteristics of writing development in kindergarten through second grade with the development of writers in third grade and above (adapted from Mooney 2005).

THE TEACHER'S ROLE IN INDEPENDENT WRITING

The teacher's role during independent writing is to gather on-going information—assessment—to determine the degree to which students have acquired skills and strategies and are now able to apply them. The teacher then uses this information to plan the future learning steps and the support that will need to be provided. The teacher questions, "How effective has the learning been? How is the learning being applied and transferred? How will I plan for next steps?" (Mooney 2005, 26). As students write independently, the teacher observes their behaviors to determine their ability to manage their own learning. The teacher also analyzes the writing that students produce during independent writing to evaluate how the learning is being applied. All of this information is used to plan future instruction. At times the teacher may use the approach of independent writing to gather summative assessment—formal assessment that is done less often to measure growth over time.

Independent Writing K-2	Independent Writing Grade 3 and Up
Develops topics from experiences with family, friends, and school	Develops topics from a greater range of interests and experiences
Talks and listens to peers about ideas for writing and receives feedback	Takes more responsibility for seeking feedback and using that feedback to improve as a writer
Draws pictures, labels pictures, makes simple lists to develop and use ideas while planning, drafting, and revising	Uses a greater variety of ways to select topics and plan for writing, such as discussion with peers, determining appropriate graphic organizers, quick writing, and revisiting previous writing
Organizes writing for sequence and with beginning, middle, and end	Organizes writing using a greater variety of organizational structures, such as comparison/contrast, cause and effect, problem/solution, or chronological
Writes for a variety of purposes, such as to inform, entertain, or request Writes in different forms such as recounts, retells, stories, procedural texts, and expository	Writes in a variety of forms according to the desired purpose
Uses what has been learned from other writers	Uses appropriate techniques, style, and text features
Revises to make meaning clear	Uses a variety of options for revisions, such as substitutions, extensions, sequence, examples, tone, and emphasis
Proofreads using what has been learned about spelling and conventions	Proofreads and uses resources to check accuracy of spelling, conventions, and usage
Develops confidence and enthusiasm for writing	Pursues writing with confidence and enthusiasm

Figure 8.1: Characteristics of writing development
Content © 2005 by Margaret E. Mooney

Observing and Assessing during Independent Writing

When students write independently, the teacher is able to gather important information about each student's writing development. The teacher can evaluate the student's understandings, skills, and attitudes to determine what learning is still being acquired and needs continued support, and she can determine what learning has been internalized to the degree that it can be applied in new areas. If students cannot yet apply the new learning, the teacher makes adjustments in future teaching to provide the support or practice that is needed.

As the teacher observes and assesses during independent writing, she will find some students eager to write and able to persevere even when they come to places in their writing that challenge them. These students quickly engage in the process of writing and work independently and collaboratively with peers, seeking feedback at appropriate times. They are confident about what they can do on their own and value feedback from others. Independent writing is used to discover ways to transfer what the writers know to new contexts and in new ways. These students are developing the attitudes, understandings, and behaviors of independent, self-improving writers.

Using the information that was gained about these students from observation during independent writing and analyzing the students' writing, the teacher plans for instruction. She decides, for example, that these students need sustained time for writing and peer conferencing to apply their learning in a new context. Their writing and their attitudes about writing indicate that it is time to step away so that these students do not become dependent on the teacher. As the teacher monitors the development of students, it is important to recognize those students who do not need as much support, but rather need more time and opportunity to apply and extend what they are learning. If the teacher does intervene, it is with the purpose of moving students to a higher stage of development.

The teacher also observes some students who are reluctant to even begin writing, having little confidence in their ability to write and rarely seeking feedback from their peers. As the teacher considers why these students are reluctant and have little confidence, she also analyzes their writing and finds that their pieces are often flat and contain mainly basic vocabulary. They do not understand how to improve as writers.

Because these students are reluctant to seek feedback from their peers during independent writing, the teacher decides that they need more opportunities to talk about their ideas as they begin to write and develop their topics. She wants them to understand why writers need to seek feedback to problem solve. The teacher decides that during guided writing these students need to focus on the topics they are choosing and discuss how they are developing their purpose for these topics. While students discuss their topics during guided writing, they also analyze how they are making decisions about their topic choice and their purpose. They discuss the role of feedback for a writer having difficulty developing a topic. The teacher helps them consider what steps they need to take to become more independent when choosing topics and what they can do if they encounter problems. The teacher recognizes that these students need to understand their

What the Teacher Discovers and Uses to Plan Instruction

responsibilities as independent writers as well as further develop strategies to problem solve.

Other students in the class may display enthusiasm as they begin writing, but quickly lose interest in their writing, or they may reach a point of struggle and decide to abandon the topic altogether rather than developing strategies to work through their problems. Analyzing these students' independent writing, the teacher sees little evidence of revision. She adjusts her plan for shared writing to demonstrate why writers make revisions and the strategies writers use to revise. She begins by showing them how a writer recognizes the places where using an example would help clarify the ideas presented. She will also show them how an example can be added into text by writing it on another page and inserting a symbol to show where the addition has been made. This shared experience includes discussion of how students will use what they have learned in their own writing. Once again the teacher considers how to support the students in developing the critical understandings of revision but also supports their understanding of how to take what they are learning into their own writing. The teacher will continue to assess the students' understandings of revision during independent writing to determine if further support is needed.

SELF-IMPROVING WRITERS

For students to become self-improving writers, they must clearly understand what they are expected to learn, why they need to learn, and how they are to learn (Clarke 2003). If the learning target is to write expository text using the structure of cause and effect, the teacher might begin by sharing models of expository text that use this text structure while reading to and writing for students. The teacher also explains and shows students how to use this organizational structure, demonstrating the thinking of a writer. The students are further supported as they acquire the new understandings of cause and effect through experiences in guided reading and writing.

During guided reading the students will have opportunities to analyze the author's use of cause and effect as an organizational structure. The discussion will also include how they will use what they are learning as they write. For example, a group of sixth-grade students worked with their teacher to practice what they were learning about cause and effect to organize their writing about their current science topic of global warming. With the teacher's guidance each student planned for his writing by identifying examples of the effects of global warming. They then discussed the causes of global warming to further develop their ideas. The discussion included how they would use this organization in their own pieces of writing about this topic. The students continued writing independently, using what they had learned about cause and effect as a way to develop and organize ideas in their writing. Students practice what they have learned in a piece of their own writing with the teacher's guidance during guided writing. This support ensures that students have had time and opportunity to develop the understandings and skills they need to use this new skill independently. These supported experiences play an important role in developing the confidence and enthusiasm to try out new learning independently. Students can then be expected to take responsibility to use cause and effect as an organizational structure in a piece of writing during their independent writing time.

During more supported approaches the students and teacher develop success criteria. The success criteria focus on the process of how the learning target will be achieved (Clarke 2003). Clear learning targets with success criteria support independence. Students know what they need to practice while working independently, how to use the new learning target, and how to self-evaluate progress.

Planning for the Development of Self-Improving Writers

Planning for the development of self-improving writers begins with the teacher's understanding of long-term planning. The long-term plan ensures coverage of content and skills of the state and district curriculum standards, giving an overview of the school year. The long-term plan is the vision of independence. It lays out what the independent learner needs to know and be able to do.

Teachers, sometimes working in a grade-level or subject-area team, use the school's long-term plan to develop a medium-term plan, which breaks the year into manageable chunks of perhaps six- or nine-week periods. They identify learning targets, considering what they know about their current group of students. They discuss resources that will be used and how the learning targets will be assessed. As they plan, the teachers describe what success toward the learning target should look and sound like both for learning and teaching. This discussion helps the teachers identify what students need to be able to do to be independent and how students will develop that independence.

The medium-term plan also includes how the learning will be assessed. The team plans for the students to set their own goals within the learning target, self-evaluate, and plan for their own next steps using success criteria. Self-evaluation and planning for learning are important aspects of being independent, self-improving writers and need to be considered during the planning process. Development of clear targets and success criteria is a necessary part

CHAPTER 8 INDEPENDENT WRITING

of medium-term planning if students are to achieve independence. The team also develops a form for the students to use for goal setting, planning for their learning, and self-evaluation of their learning. Figure 8.2 is an example of a goal-setting form.

With the medium-term plan as a framework, each teacher plans daily. These short-term plans allow the teacher to consider what students have learned and the next steps that need to be taken by the class and by individuals.

Name: _____

My Strengths as a Writer
I can use descriptive language when I write stories to paint a picture in the reader's mind.
I plan for my writing using notes and graphic organizers.
I reread my writing to revise and make the meaning clear.

My Goals
1. I will use descriptive language as a persuasive technique.
2. I will think about my word choice (adjectives, adverbs and verbs) when I revise.
3. I will use visual language in informational writing.

How will I accomplish my goals?
I will think about the picture I want to describe for the reader.
I will think about the kinds of words that will create that picture.
I will read brochures and pay attention to the author's word choice. I will look at the kinds of visual language an author uses in informational text. I will need to read my writing to my classmates and ask, "Does it paint a picture with words?"

What have I learned?
I can read what other authors write and learn more about writing. I need to ask other writers to listen to my writing and ask questions that will help me know where there are gaps in my writing. A thesaurus helps me use more interesting words.

Figure 8.2: Student goal-setting form
Form © 2006 by Mary Ann Whitfield

Time for independent writing is part of the daily plan. Some days may provide longer periods for sustained independent writing, but on other days students may need to receive more support and have less time to write independently. It is up to the teacher to maintain the balance of support, taking into consideration how to build up longer times for sustained writing for all students.

The following is an example of how a team of seventh-grade teachers incorporates independent writing into their classroom instruction through long-term, medium-term, and short-term planning. The seventh-grade team uses the school's long-term plan as they develop a six-week medium-term plan. Expectations stated in the long-term plan are that students will identify the author's purpose in different types of text and that they will write for a variety of purposes in a variety of forms. During the current six-week term, the seventh-grade team decides to focus on the writer's purpose to influence or persuade. While discussing resources, the team identifies brochures as the form they will use to develop their students' understandings of how writers use persuasion to influence their readers in informational text. Using brochures as a resource, they plan how they will provide opportunities for students to learn to read critically and recognize when the author's purpose is to persuade. The teachers will help their students learn that as readers they must evaluate and make judgments when reading persuasive text. These understandings of reading will help them as they learn about persuasive techniques and how they need to think as writers whose purpose is to persuade.

During guided reading the students will analyze brochures to understand the techniques that writers employ to persuade, such as using descriptive language. They will consider how writers use visual language, such as charts, graphs, diagrams, illustrations, and other text features, as well as written language to influence the thinking of their readers. The teachers know that these reading experiences will help their students understand how writers apply what they know about oral, written, and visual language to persuade. Students will be expected to apply these understandings and skills during independent writing.

As the result of these reading experiences, the students will work with their teacher to develop success criteria for persuasive writing. Success criteria provide a tool for self-evaluation and give the students a valuable resource to support their independence. They will know what understandings and skills they are expected to apply as they practice persuasive writing in informational text and evaluate the effectiveness of their writing. Through careful planning based on curriculum standards and the assessed learning needs of each student, the teachers ensure that students have a learning target that is

An Example of Developing Independent Writers through Planning

manageable, experiences and resources to support their learning, and a tool for self-evaluation and planning.

Once the success criteria have been developed, students will be asked to write their own brochures during independent writing. Students will choose their own topics for the brochures and use their new understanding of persuasion as they write the brochures independently. Each student will write a brochure, and there will be opportunities for discussion and peer feedback. The teacher will plan for some of these discussions to occur during guided writing to support students in understanding how to receive and provide feedback. Students will also be expected to seek feedback from peers as they write independently.

The focus of the teacher's assessment and the students' self-assessment is the use of persuasion in informational text. Each student will use the success criteria that were developed by the class to plan their writing and evaluate the brochure he or she develops. Their evaluation is not just of the product of the brochure, but it is an evaluation to determine what each student has learned about persuasion and can now apply independently.

Figure 8.3 is an example of a chart of the success criteria that the teacher develops with students. The chart is displayed in the classroom to serve as a

Learning Target: **Use persuasion in a brochure**

Success Criteria: **Use persuasive language (written language)**

Examples:
   Superlatives
   Emotive language
   Comparisons
   Opinion
   Description

Use illustrative and graphic material as a technique to persuade (visual language)

Use the layout of the brochure as a technique to persuade (visual language)

Figure 8.3: Learning target and success criteria
Content adapted from *Text Forms and Features,* page 27 and
© 2001 by Margaret E. Mooney

reminder of what is being learned and what the learner needs to do to be successful. Students use the chart as they are planning, drafting, and revising their brochures and to assess the effectiveness of their use of persuasion.

During the approach of independent writing students will be practicing what they have learned about persuasive writing and brochures. The texts they use during their reading experiences will serve as models for them as they apply their understandings of persuasion in writing and evaluate their effectiveness.

As they write, students will be assessing their effectiveness in using their new understandings of persuasive writing. The success criteria the class developed (Figure 8.3) will be important as they evaluate their brochures and consider how they will improve this piece of writing and improve as writers.

In addition to the medium-term plan, each teacher will use the assessment gathered during independent writing to determine the students' strengths and their next learning steps. This information is used to plan day to day, making the learning and teaching manageable.

In a seventh-grade classroom, students were writing brochures. Their teacher carefully observed as they worked independently on this writing project. She recognized that many of the students did not understand how to use the success criteria to evaluate their writing. A number of students did not seek feedback from classmates when considering what revisions they needed to make and in fact did little revision. The teacher then decided that the class would need more demonstration and guided practice in how to use the success criteria. Some students were having difficulty using persuasive language. The teacher realized she needed to provide more supported experiences for these students. Those students needed to work in a small group with the teacher's support to analyze how writers use descriptive language. The teacher provided text with good examples of description for the students to consider how the author used descriptive language. During this instruction students made some revisions to their brochures focusing on the use of descriptive language. They continued making revisions independently, practicing what they had learned in their guided group.

An Example from One Teacher's Classroom

For the few students who were not managing time well, the teacher scheduled time to check with these students during independent writing to make sure they understand the expectations and were taking responsibility for their work.

Figure 8.4 is an example of a teacher's daily plan that resulted from what she had learned about her students through on-going assessment.

Whole Group

Discussion/Reflection:

What have we learned about using persuasion in the brochures we are writing? What is going well?

What problems do we have? How can we solve problems as we work independently?

Whole Group Demonstration

Objective: Evaluate the use of persuasive language using the success criteria

Resource: Draft of a brochure that the teacher has created

Approach: Demonstrate a writing conference using a fishbowl experience (conference with a group of 6 students while the rest of the class watches). Does my use of descriptive language create images that will appeal to the reader of my brochure?

Independent Writing/Reading

Students work on their brochures. Some students are writing, some are conferencing with peers, and some are analyzing brochures and other informational text to better understand the techniques writers use to persuade.

Rove

Students to Observe:

Peter (Is he staying focused? If not, why not?)

Jennifer (Is she interacting with other students to get feedback? Does she need encouragement to seek help from peers?)

Carlos (How is he using the resources he identified yesterday as examples of good descriptive language to help him revise a section of his brochure? Can he do this independently or does he need further support?)

Carolyn, Shaneeka, and José (Do they understand how to use the success criteria?)

Small Group

Objective: To use layout as a persuasive technique

Group: Anita, Eric, Hector, Jeremy, Esperanza, Leeza, Paul, Analee, Ana

Resource: Brochures

Approach: What has the writer and illustrator included in the layout and why? How is the visual language organized to support the written text? What visual language will you include? How will you organize the layout of your brochure?

Rove

Observe: Are students able to use their new understandings and skills independently? Who still needs support?

Small Group

Objective: Use detailed description as a technique to persuade

Group: Elizabeth, Dana, Jake, Shawna, Ralph, Pedro, Darrin, Burt

Resource: Students' brochures

Approach: Each writer identifies a place in his or her brochure where detailed description was used and reads that section to the group. How does the description help persuade? What suggestions do you have for the writer to consider?

Whole Group

Individual and group reflection using success criteria: What have I done well? What has been challenging? What is my plan for tomorrow?

Figure 8.4: Teacher's lesson plan
Form © 2006 by Mary Ann Whitfield

Name:

Genre/Form	Date	Strengths/Next Steps	New Understandings, Skills, and Strategies
Expository/article	10/10	S–Analyzes published writing to understand writer's techniques Accepts feedback from peers NS–Use text features such a title, headings, diagram, and so on to write expository text	Plans for and uses a variety of text features in expository text

Figure 8.5: Monitoring form for genre/text form
Form © 2006 by Mary Ann Whitfield

To assess students' independence teachers will not only need to assess their day-to-day learning, but also their learning over time. Students will need to learn to write in a variety of genres and develop the traits of a good writer. Figures 8.5 and 8.6 are two types of forms a teacher might use to monitor student's progress over time.

ORGANIZING AND MANAGING INDEPENDENT WRITING
The Essential Skills provide a framework as the teacher organizes and plans for independent writing (Ministry of Education 1993).

During independent writing students take responsibility for managing their own learning. Self-management skills are critical for the development of independence and are part of the teacher's planning process. By making learning targets clear and helping students identify and use success criteria, the teacher helps students to develop independence in managing their own learning. Learners need to be able to set and use goals as a focus when they work independently so they can assess progress and make needed

Monitoring Student Progress over Time

Self-Management Skills

Name:

Traits	Date	Strengths/Next Steps	New Understanding, Skills, and Strategies
Ideas and Content			
Organization	10/20	S-Plans using prior knowledge about topic Takes notes from several sources NS-Organize notes to plan for expository writing	Gathers, selects and organizes ideas for informational writing Uses cause and effect as an organizational structure
Sentence Fluency			
Voice			
Word Choice			
Conventions			

Figure 8.6: Monitoring form for writing traits
Form © 2006 by Mary Ann Whitfield

improvements. These improvements are not just about improving a piece of writing, but rather they are about the student improving as a writer, developing skills and understandings that they can use in the future. Students should understand that their goal is to apply what they have internalized in new and different ways.

Students are expected to take responsibility for managing their time both during class and over longer periods of time so that they complete their writing assignments in a timely and efficient manner. One way of helping students learn to manage time is through the use of daily planners. These planners can take the form of calendars in which the students record due dates set by the teacher and dates that the students set for themselves to help them break longer tasks into more manageable time periods. Students may find it helpful to spend a little time each day planning what they need to accomplish during their independent time. Teachers must recognize that they need to trust their students to take responsibility while showing them how to manage their learning.

Organizing personal writing materials is another important aspect of self-management. Because both the students and the teacher will need to evaluate learning over time, the students' writing should be housed so that the writing is not lost. Composition books, spiral notebooks, or binders work well for this purpose. When student writing is written on loose sheets of notebook paper without a specific place to house them, the writing might be lost. Students need to understand the value of their work and learn the importance of taking care of their materials. The teacher plans how these self-organization and self-management skills will be taught and their development monitored. Students need to see models for organization, just as they need models of good writing. The teacher needs to demonstrate the thinking of a writer who understands how to organize materials and why organization is important. Goals for organization are needed as well as success criteria. Some students need more support in developing the organizational skills they need to be independent learners.

To develop as writers, students must learn to be able to solve the problems that writers encounter by thinking critically and creatively. As they learn how to think as writers, they need to recognize their challenges and have strategies to solve them. During independent writing, teachers should trust their students to wrestle with problems they encounter, knowing that during shared and guided writing their students have been supported in learning how to think as writers. Students will practice using what they have learned about the process of writing to help them apply what they have learned about text forms and features to make appropriate decisions.

Problem Solving, Communication, and Work and Study Skills

The independent writing time is organized so that students not only work by themselves but also have the opportunity to conference with peers. Giving and receiving feedback is crucial to solving problems. Oral language provides the foundation for writing, so it is necessary for teachers to ensure that students are able to talk with their peers during this time and learn to be purposeful as they talk. Students may need to talk through their thinking as they plan to generate and organize their ideas or to hear what their writing sounds like by reading it orally to peers who will help the writer make revisions. These kinds of interactions help the learners develop their communication skills, as they must learn to listen carefully and given constructive responses. Since talk is an important element in the learning process, the teacher helps students learn appropriate voice levels during independent work times. This teaching involves modeling and demonstrating what independent writing looks and sounds like. It also involves practice and self-evaluation by the students.

The teacher shows students how to conference with peers during guided writing experiences so that they understand their role and responsibilities during independent conferences. The writers need to know that it is their responsibility to be prepared for these conferences with their peers. They need to come prepared to share the purpose for their writing and where in their writing they feel they need help. The students who provide the feedback must understand how to listen and provide constructive ideas. It is not their responsibility to tell the writer what to write, but rather to ask questions that will help the writer consider how to make meaning clear or explain where they felt the writing lacked clarity and why.

The teacher considers also how the time and space in the classroom is organized to encourage interaction. Will students be able to ask for feedback any time they need it, or will there be times that they are expected to work alone, with a time scheduled for interaction? If students are to have the opportunity to meet with peers, the teacher will need to plan for the arrangement of furniture that will encourage these kinds of discussions. The teacher and students need a procedure for setting up conferences for feedback. The class could use a white board to do daily scheduling. The teacher posts the names of students who will meet together that day in a teacher-led guided writing lesson and for individual conferences. There could be a place on the white board for students to sign up requesting a conference with the teacher. There also would need to be a place on the white board for students to post their names if they want to schedule a conference with peers. Those students would include the names of one or more peers from whom they want feedback.

Information Skills

Resources such as the thesaurus, dictionary, computer, examples of good writing, and so on need to be available to students during independent writing. Students will receive instruction in how writers use these resources during the other instructional approaches, and they will have time to practice using them as part of their independent writing experience.

Observing, Reflecting, Assessing, and Planning

Just as teachers assess the development of students' writing during this approach, they assess their students' application of the Essential Skills. For students to be successful in acquiring these skills they must be clear about what they are and what they mean. As the school year begins, the teacher plans how these skills will be introduced and taught. Early discussions with the class need to involve the students in setting the expectations in regard to these skills so that they develop a sense of ownership and responsibility. Often teachers give students a long list of what they are supposed to do, but by making the students aware of these skills and involving them in planning for how they will be developed, students are better able to take the responsibility expected of them. Once again it is important that teachers trust their students and give them opportunities to apply these skills.

ATTAINING THE GOAL OF INDEPENDENCE

Students will attain the goal of independence when they have many opportunities to write independently with clear understandings of their role and responsibilities. These experiences of working without the support of the teacher put students in charge of their learning, giving them power and control of language. They experience the freedom to apply their understandings and skills, which leads to the ability to extend what they know and are able to do as writers. As students become self-improving learners, they learn how to focus their personal targets within the class targets, evaluate their learning, recognizing strengths and next learning steps, and plan for their own learning.

Weaving the Magic Together: Threads of Student Success and Engagement

Terrell Young is a professor of literacy education at Washington State University, where he teaches a variety of undergraduate and graduate courses in children's literature and reading. Terry taught elementary school for twelve years in Wyoming, Utah, and Venezuela. He is the past president of both the Washington Organization for Reading Development and the IRA Children's Literature and Reading Special Interest Group and the current president of the NCTE Children's Literature Assembly. He co-authored the books *Literature-Based Instruction with English Language Learners, K-12* (Allyn & Bacon, 2002) and *What Every Teacher Should Know about English Language Learners* (Allyn & Bacon, 2004), edited *Happily Ever After: Sharing Folk Literature with Elementary and Middle School Students* (IRA, 2004), and co-edited *Supporting the Literacy Development of English Learners: Increasing Success in All Classrooms* (IRA, 2006). He is blessed to be married to a wonderful elementary music teacher and to have four terrific kids to remind him of his imperfections.

	Desired Outcome	Student's Activity and Thinking	Support/Guidance	Teacher's Role	Approach
PART 1	Self-awareness	Observing Listening Absorbing *There is something in this for me. I want to be able to do likewise.*	Support	Modeling and inspiring Showing benefits of a skilled reader/writer in action	Read to or write for
PART 2	Self-correcting	Absorbing and practicing alongside a more knowledge-able other *I want to try to do this. I can practice with someone else.*	Support and guidance	Demonstrating— explicitly explaining— the "how" as well as the "what" to encourage participation	Shared reading/ writing
PART 3	Self-assessing	Practicing and applying in other contexts *I can apply what I have learned as I practice by myself with someone watching and guiding me. I can overcome challenges by thinking about what I am learning. The more I practice, the easier it becomes.*	Guidance	Monitoring through interactive forma-tive assessment (nurturing rather than measuring), questioning, provok-ing, focusing on how meaning is accessed	Guided reading/ writing
PART 4	Self-improving	Gaining confidence in applying learning and meeting new challenges in self-selected contexts. *I can use what I have learned in other contexts. I can think about ways I can improve. I can use what I have learned to learn new things.*	Guidance and reflection	Observing, assess-ing through formal formative and perhaps some sum-mative procedures, measuring effective-ness of learning and application Planning next learn-ing target and learn-ing opportunities	Independent reading/ writing

Weaving the Magic Together: Threads of Student Success and Engagement

by Terrell A. Young

Everyone wants to see high levels of literacy for students, especially those in Grades 3 through 8. However, what meets the requirements for this level of literacy differs among educators. For some people, high test scores will suffice. These individuals will not consider the fact that some students receive high reading and writing scores on tests but rarely choose to read and write. To others, achievement scores contribute only a small part of what they consider in highly literate behavior. Instead, they seek literacy engagement which, according to Guthrie, contains two common threads. First, students are actively involved in reading and writing. Second, engaged reading and writing are more about the deep thinking and strategy use involved in writing to communicate or learning from text than merely completing assignments (2004). The aim of this book is to help teachers create engaged writers and readers.

Such students would use literacy for many purposes. Literacy would have a powerful impact on what they do, what they know, and who they are. As students progress through the grades, it is likely that "ongoing literacy development is a more challenging task than ensuring excellent reading education in the primary grades, for two reasons: first, the literacy skills are more complex, more embedded in subject matters and more multiply determined; second, [the students] are not as universally motivated to read better or as interested in school-based reading as kindergartners" (Biancarosa and Snow 2004, 1–2).

Likewise, a recent RAND Reading Study Group Report noted, "Research has shown that many children who read at the third grade level in grade three will not automatically become proficient comprehenders in later grades" (Snow 2002, xxi). Yet, literacy development in Grades 3 through 8 is obtainable. Just as beautiful tapestries take skill, planning, materials, and effort to weave, classrooms where highly literate and engaged students thrive have many similar components. These components include teachers, resources, classroom environment, time, and approaches. Moreover, there is an interaction between and among components. For example, the teacher's role is crucial to the development of the learning environment and the implementation of the approaches.

THE TEACHER

A resurgence of political interest in commercial programs has led to more faith in and mandates for prescribed curriculum. While materials **do** matter, teachers are really what make a difference. The now-classic First Grade Studies of the 1960s concluded that "regardless of the quality of a program, resource, or strategy, it is the teacher and learning situation that make a difference" (Bond and Dykstra 1997). Researchers have repeatedly noted that teacher quality and expertise consistently and accurately predicts student achievement (Darling-Hammond 2000; Snow 2002).

How much credit can teachers take for their students' learning? Quite a bit! Ronald Ferguson (1991) determined that 48% of the variance in student achievement could be attributed to home and family factors that are largely out of the school system's control. Yet, teachers can claim credit for 43% of student learning. While this amount is impressive, New Zealand educators suggest that a teacher's influence can even be greater: "Our best evidence is that what happens in classrooms through quality teaching and through the quality of the learning environment generated by the teacher and students, is the key variable in explaining up to 59%, or even more, of the variance in student scores" (Ministry of Education 2003, 8). No matter the political climate and views on schooling, teachers frequently need to be reminded that it is what they do and how they teach their students that matters most; it is teachers, not programs, that make a difference.

Richard Allington and Peter Johnston noted qualities in fourth-grade teachers whose students were highly literate. These students' "literateness" was determined by more than achievement. It also involved what they did and what they were becoming as they developed "literate identities and relationships" and cultivated values and beliefs (2002, 189). The teachers' qualities that contributed to their students' literate ways were consistent with findings of other studies.

Effective teachers have similar personality traits and characteristics:

■ Warm, caring, supportive, encouraging, friendly, genuinely likes people, trusting, respectful, and nonjudgmental

■ Enthusiastic, enjoys work

■ Sense of agency[1], confidence

■ Accurate self-assessment (Allington and Johnston 2002).

These traits manifest themselves in teachers who drew attention to the positive in their interactions with students. They expressed interest in the students' lives and ways of thinking. Instruction was organized to engage students and encourage student self-management.

Likewise, these teachers possessed certain beliefs, attitudes, and expectations that contributed to the interactions with students and classroom environment and tone, as well as instruction:

■ Expects diversity

■ Assumes potential

■ Learning is social

■ Learning requires ownership, relevance, choice

■ Error is important

■ Modeling is important (Allington and Johnston 2002).

These beliefs, attitudes, and expectations greatly influence all forms of classroom interaction and create the underpinnings of the classroom environment—both the physical and emotional environment. Moreover, the teachers' beliefs will determine the role resources play in students' reading and writing.

Similarly, being writers and readers is also important. For example, teachers' reading habits significantly affect student achievement, motivation, and engagement (Applegate and Applegate 2004). Timothy Morrison, James

---

[1] *Teachers demonstrate a sense of agency when they possess a firm understanding of literacy and realize that their intentional selection of strategies and approaches has an impact on their students' learning.*

Jacobs, and William Swinyard conducted research through which they found that teachers who are enthusiastic readers are more likely to use recommended innovations in their teaching than their peers who are not passionate readers (1999). Thus, it seems obvious that passionate adult readers and writers are better suited to help students become thoughtful engaged writers and readers than those who do not enjoy reading and writing themselves.

INSTRUCTION

Engaged writers and readers need strategy instruction that will help them develop thoughtful literacy; a literacy that enables them to think deeply about their reading and writing. One student noted, "I used to read like a water skier skimming across the surface. Now, I read like a scuba diver." His teacher, a member of a *Mosaic of Thought* study group (Keene and Zimmermann 1997), had taught him strategies in a profoundly different way that enabled him to plumb the depths of text.

Typically, exemplary teachers focus on only a few comprehension strategies. These strategies generally include some of the following: building background and making connections, constructing mental images, predicting/inferring, determining importance, questioning, summarizing/synthesizing, monitoring, and evaluation (Allington 2006; Keene and Zimmermann 1997; Oczkus 2004). Teachers are most effective when comprehension instruction includes "teacher explanations and modeling of strategies, with scaffolded student practice in strategies application over a long period of time" (Pressley 2002, 280). Often the guided practice or scaffolding takes place in small groups or with partners involving "student conversations, rich in student reports of how they are applying strategies and their interpretations of texts being read. Long-term participation in such groups is intended to produce internalization of the strategic processes" (Pressley 2002, 280).

Sometimes the strategies are combined to create "strategy packages." A case in point is reciprocal teaching that combines four of the strategies used by good readers to comprehend text: predicting, questioning, clarifying, and summarizing (Palincsar and Brown 1984). Researchers found that the combination of the strategies was even more powerful than teaching the strategies independently. Oczkus (2003) provides teachers with an excellent resource for learning more about incorporating reciprocal teaching into their teaching routines via whole group instruction, guided reading, or literature circles.

As stated above, conversation plays a huge role in the development of reading comprehension. Ann Ketch notes that "conversation is a basis for critical thinking. It is the thread that ties together cognitive strategies and provides students with the practice that becomes the foundation for reading, writing, and thinking" (2005, 8). When conversing about commonly read text, students can hear differing viewpoints. Hearing these viewpoints "increases students' understanding, memory, and monitoring of [their] own thinking" (Ketch 2005, 9–10). Student achievement and motivation are typically higher when students have opportunities to interact with their classmates and converse about their reading (Guthrie and Humenick 2004; Taylor, Pressley, and Pearson 2002).

APPROACHES

Many researchers have noted that effective teachers provide scaffolded instruction, in which "teachers give high support for students practicing new [strategies] and then slowly decreasing that support to increase student ownership and self-sufficiency" (Biancarosa and Snow 2004, 14). Thus, student independence is the goal and measure of teacher success. The models of reading and writing to and for, shared reading and writing, guided reading and writing, and independent reading and writing ideally gradually turn more and more responsibility from the teachers to the students.

Teachers who use these modeled strategies of reading and writing to and for students provide their students with maximum support (Mooney 1990). Reading and writing to and for students allows teachers to model for their students; students have an opportunity to see proficient writers and readers modeling strategies.

Reading and Writing To and For Students

In shared reading and writing, students receive the support needed to be successful in activities they could not do independently. Appropriate for both whole and small group experiences, the shared approaches allow students to join in strategies in a comfortable and safe context. These approaches allow students to unpack the processes and prepare them to take more responsibility with teacher support.

Shared Reading and Writing

Miller (this volume) notes that sometimes students learn about a strategy, skill, form, or procedure in a demonstration but do not have the depth of understanding to actually apply what they have learned in their own reading and writing. The shared approaches provide some students with an opportunity to learn the skills at such depth that they can utilize them in their own work. For others, additional scaffolding will be necessary through the guided approaches.

CONCLUSION

Guided Reading and Writing

The guided approaches for reading and writing enable students to "have a go" at certain skills, strategies, forms, or materials with teacher support. While guided reading is generally done with small groups, guided writing might be applied in a whole- or small-group context. For example, an entire class may need some support as they continue to write to given prompts while only a few students need additional help in revising for sentence fluency or word choice.

A note of caution: during guided instruction too many teachers keep students dependent upon them and their support to complete the task at hand. Effective teachers only provide support when needed, while less effective teachers control the students' reading and writing.

Independent Reading and Writing

For far too many students, limited desirable literacy activity takes place outside of the classroom. For these students, instructional activities represent the only opportunities for them to read and write (Snow 2002). Likewise, independent reading during class is often discontinued after the primary grades. Students who do not read "may have difficulty engaging and profiting from the broad array of expository and technical texts encountered in school learning, even if [they] have no basic intellectual deficits or basic deficits in reading or oral language development" (Snow 2002, 23).

Moreover, it is the independent approaches that provide students the opportunities to practice the full acts of reading and writing (Cunningham and Allington 2003). While mini-lessons may focus on writing effective leads, writing with voice, or synthesizing information, independent reading and writing provide students with an opportunity to apply the skills and strategies they have learned through the other approaches. This time is critically important for students' success as readers and writers. Guthrie notes that it is often the amount of practice that distinguishes an expert reader or writer from a novice (2004).

Effective teachers "monitor and encourage" students as they engage in independent reading and writing (Stahl 2004). Authors in this volume have illustrated how teachers can monitor what students do in reading and writing and what teachers can do to hold them accountable for the skills and strategies that they have learned in the shared and guided approaches.

THE PHYSICAL ENVIRONMENT

The classroom (and school) environment should clearly exhibit the importance and value of reading and writing and celebrate students' literacy accomplishments. This emphasis on print includes: prominent displays of students' written work for peers to read and discuss, students' written and artistic responses to reading, and bulletin boards with postings of the class's favorite books alongside student recommendations and reviews. Displays spotlighting a particular author's work, implementation of stylistic devices, and actual books as well as "real world" print materials linked to current units of study spark student interest and curiosity.

Centers supplied with materials (such as index cards, self-stick notes, message pads, paper of assorted sizes and colors, notepads, envelopes, postcards, stationery, pens, pencils, markers, and so on) for writing and also for responding to reading promote student involvement with text. Finally, room furniture can be arranged to promote small-group interaction, to provide greater student-level access to books and other literacy materials, and to encourage independent reading, writing, and learning. More and more teachers are recognizing that their classrooms do not have to look like sterile institutions; they can provide homey touches such as couches, lamps, and rugs that help students feel positive, comfortable, and motivated to learn (Hadaway, Vardell, and Young 2002).

CLASSROOM LIBRARIES

One essential factor of getting students to read independently is access to books. Students are likely to spend more time reading when they are in classrooms with adequate classroom libraries (Allington and Cunningham 2001). Interviews with avid readers have found that children who love to read almost always have access to books at home. Since many students today do not have that access, it is paramount that **all** children be provided with books in the classroom (Fractor et al. 1993).

Classroom libraries provide students with immediate access to books; they can provide teachers with the opportunity to put the right book in a student's hands at a moment's notice. Students who have ready access to books in their classrooms have better attitudes about reading, reading achievement, and comprehension than their peers with less access to books in the classroom. Moreover, students are likely to spend more time reading when they are in classrooms with adequate classroom libraries (Allington and Cunningham 1996; Krashen 1998; Routman 2003). For example, Leslie Morrow (2003) and Susan Neuman (1999) both note that students read 50 to 60 percent more in classrooms with libraries than in classrooms without them.

This increase in voluntary reading can contribute to gains in reading achievement. In a study of 32 schools in Maryland, for example, Guthrie, Schafer,

Von Secker, and Alban (2000) found that an abundance of trade books in the classroom predicted gains on state-wide reading, writing, and science tests. According to Krashen (2004), more books in the classroom leads to more voluntary reading, which in turn results in higher achievement. This increased volume of voluntary reading is critical because students who score well on standardized reading tests read far more outside of school than students who perform poorly on such tests (Anderson, Wilson, and Fielding 1988).

Of late, more and more experts have noted the importance of providing students with access to nonfiction texts. Many reports highlight the value of including nonfiction texts in the classroom library (Young, Moss, and Cornwell n.d.). First, such books can effectively address student interests in ways that stories cannot. Secondly, they can increase student domain knowledge in a variety of areas, thereby leading to increased levels of background knowledge. Nonfiction is often the preferred genre of many students—especially boys (Smith and Wilhelm 2002). Furthermore, reading more nonfiction can lead to higher reading achievement (Routman 2003). On the contrary, students with little experience with nonfiction have difficulty comprehending such text and fail to determine the important information located within (Stoodt-Hill and Amspaugh-Corson 2005).

Shelley Harwayne, the well-known literacy consultant and administrator, notes, "No matter the grade level, when I walk in and out of classrooms, I expect to see classroom libraries brimming with nonfiction texts" (1999, 24). All too often, however, classroom libraries contain little nonfiction literature (Stead 2001). According to Harvey Daniels, "language arts teachers have done a great job of hooking kids on all kinds of novels . . . but students also need to engage with the nonfiction genres that represent 84% of adult, real world text (and a similar percentage of the reading passages of high stakes standardized tests)" (2004, 44).

Moss suggests that, "About half the collection should be devoted to engaging information books and biographies, and this percentage should increase as children move through the grades. Some books should be pertinent to classroom topics of study, while others should have a broader appeal. Students can use these books for voluntary reading, in inquiry study, reference, or for browsing" (2002, 63).

Effective classroom libraries are organized to support student book choice and engagement (Sibberson and Szymusiak 2003). Some teachers choose to locate nonfiction in another part of the classroom to remind students that stories are different from factual information. However the library collection is organized, it is critical that students understand how the books are organized. Some books may be placed with covers facing outward, while others have only the spines showing. Some books are organized by genres, while the nonfiction books are generally separated by topic and the shelves or tubs are labeled accordingly.

MATERIALS

Teachers often face many obstacles when it comes to selecting materials for their students. Some teachers are required to use the adopted basal readers and textbooks. Others use a combination of trade books and the adopted curriculum materials. Still others are free to use whatever available materials they choose.

Making books available that are likely to interest and engage students is crucial and can lead to marked changes in how students view both books and themselves as readers (Samway and Whang 1995). Wise teachers learn about their students' interests and use that information to strike a balance between what students like to read and what teachers would choose for them to read. Teachers typically want their students to read books of high literary quality, while their students would make other selections (Worthy, Broaddus, and Ivey 2001). For instance, students often prefer comics, magazines, funny books, scary books, and series books to the books that teachers make available for them to read (Worthy, Moorman, and Turner 1999).

Reading suffers when students have a steady diet of books that are too hard for them; the same can be said for books that do not interest them (Allington 2006; Routman 1999). On the other hand, reading books that are too easy can result in boredom. Students generally like reading books that present a slight challenge. Engaging students in texts they find interesting is paramount. Researchers note that students' motivation, achievement, and comprehension increase when they read what is of interest to them or that relates to their own experiences (Guthrie and Humenick 2004).

For these reasons, leveled books provide students with short text they can often read in a few settings that will provide them with a sufficient challenge without overwhelming them. The leveled text should be available on topics to support the curriculum and topics of student interest. In classrooms that use a single anthology or basal, students do not get sufficient reading practice (Allington 2006). Students have more reading options and opportunities to read when teachers add leveled text and trade books to the mix.

Yet, it is not enough to have a classroom stocked with a literature anthology and leveled books. Many students in Grade 3 and beyond have not yet developed reading stamina. They do not have the reading energy to stick with a piece until they are hooked, and they have difficulty completing trade books. Therefore, novels and nonfiction chapter books are essential in every classroom. In some cases, the support provided in novel studies or literature circles will be enough for students to develop such stamina. Yet for other students, teachers will need to carefully monitor their independent reading. Teachers can help students see what types of books are easy for them to "stick with" through completion.

Many teachers note that many of their students re-read books or certain genres over and over. These students are passionate readers when reading a certain type of book, yet they are hesitant to try other books. Wise teachers help students find other books that they will also enjoy. An example can be found with the Harry Potter books. Teachers can create a space for books labeled "If you liked Harry Potter, then you will like these books." Books to include would be the Charlie Bone books by Jenny Nimmo, the Artemis Fowl books by Eoin Colfer, the Bartimaeus Trilogy by Jonathan Stroud, and *The Lightning Thief* by Rick Riordan (2005) (Figure 9.1). These titles present a range of difficulty levels and many have lots of boy appeal.

It is not enough for students to keep reading the same types of books. For some it will be fantasy, and others will prefer humorous stories, nonfiction choices, mysteries, sports fiction, or romance novels. It is the teacher's job to nudge students into new genres and reading experiences. Much of this can happen through the teacher reading aloud and literature circles. Some teachers use reading conferences as a venue for their students to set goals for expanding their reading selections and strategies.

All students need to read books that they enjoy and understand in a number of genres. Too often instruction focuses solely on fiction, and the skills do not always transfer to nonfiction literature and textbooks. Reading nonfiction trade books or content area textbooks taps into different content and strategies than what are required to comprehend fiction stories. Narrative typically revolves around a story grammar that notes setting, characters, the characters' problems or goals, characters' attempts to deal with their goals or problems, and the resolution or ending. On the other hand, comprehending nonfiction is dependent upon specific content knowledge, understanding of nonfiction text structure, and interest. Nonfiction text is organized in various text structures–sequence, cause and effect, comparison/contrast, problem/ solution, question and answer, description, and definition with examples.

If you liked Harry Potter, then you will like these books!

Artemis Fowl
series by Eoin Colfer

- *Artemis Fowl* (2001)
- *The Arctic Incident* (2002)
- *The Eternity Code* (2003)
- *The Artemis Fowl Files: The Ultimate Guide to the Best-Selling Series* (2004)
- *The Opal Deception* (2005)

Children of the Red King
series by Jenny Nimmo

- *Midnight for Charlie Bone* (2002)
- *Charlie Bone and the Time Twister* (2003)
- *Charlie Bone and the Invisible Boy* (2004)
- *Charlie Bone and the Castle of Mirrors* (2005)

The Bartimaeus Trilogy
by Jonathan Stroud

- *The Amulet of Samarkand* (2003)
- *The Golem's Eye* (2004)
- *Ptolemy's Gate* (2005)

Percy Jackson and the Olympians
adventure series by Rick Riordan

- *The Lightning Thief* (2005)
- *The Sea of Monsters* (2006)

Figure 9.1: Linking students' interests to additional texts
For complete publication information, please see References—Children's Books

Given the ever-increasing range of reading and writing levels beyond the primary grades, it is crucial that students have access to books available from a wide range of levels on the same themes and topics (Biancarosa and Snow 2004; Gambrell and Mazzoni 1999). By creating thematic and topical collections, students can read different books and still contribute to class discussions. When dealing with topical text sets, teachers often lead students in constructing data-retrieval charts or semantic maps so all of the students can make genuine contributions to class discussions and learning. An example of a nonfiction text set appears in Figure 9.2.

Poetry should play a prominent role in every classroom. Poetry is often featured on standardized tests, so students need opportunities to regularly read, write, and respond to poetry across grade levels. Many teachers also

Lewis and Clark Text Set

Adler, David. *A Picture Book of Lewis and Clark.* (2003)

Adler, David. *A Picture Book of Sacagawea.* (2001)

Blumberg, Rhoda. *The Incredible Journey of Lewis and Clark.* (1987)

Blumberg, Rhoda. *What's the Deal? Jefferson, Napoleon, and the Louisiana Purchase.* (1998)

Blumberg, Rhoda. *York's Adventures with Lewis and Clark: An African-American's Part in the Great Expedition.* (2004)

Erdrich, Liselotte. *Sacagawea.* (2003)

Morley, Jacqueline. *Across America: The Story of Lewis and Clark.* (1998)

Murphy, Claire Rudolph. *I Am Sacagawea, I Am York: Our Journey West with Lewis and Clark.* (2005)

Patent, Dorothy Hinshaw. *Animals on the Trail with Lewis and Clark.* (2002)

Patent, Dorothy Hinshaw. *Plants on the Trail with Lewis and Clark.* (2003)

Santella, Andrew. *Lewis and Clark.* (2001)

Schanzer, Rosalyn. *How We Crossed the West: The Adventures of Lewis and Clark.* (2002)

Stein, R. Conrad. *Lewis and Clark.* (1997)

Sullivan, George. *Lewis and Clark (In Their Own Words).* (1999)

Figure 9.2: A diverse collection of texts on the same topic
For complete publication information, please see References—Children's Books

Teacher Choice	Managed Choice	Student Choice
■ Core books ■ Read aloud ■ Shared reading ■ Guided reading	■ Literature circles ■ Independent reading ■ Text sets as part of thematic or content area units	■ Sustained silent reading ■ Readers' workshop

Figure 9.3: Balancing teacher and student choices for reading

note that poetry is a powerful tool for introducing and extending content area subjects. Even more important, numerous students thrive on this genre. Some collections to consider are Lori Marie Carlson's *Red Hot Salsa: Bilingual Poems on Being Young and Latino in the United States* (2005), Pat Mora's *My Own True Name* (2000), Naomi Shihab Nye's *A Maze Me: Poems for Girls* (2005), Cynthia Rylant's *Boris* (2005), Joyce Sidman's *Song of the Water Boatman & Other Pond Poems* (2005), and Gary Soto's *Worlds Apart: Traveling with Fernie and Me* (2005).

CHOICE

Guthrie and Humenick note that providing choice in reading results in increased comprehension, interest in reading, and time spent reading (2004). Effective teachers provide a balance of teacher and student choice, as illustrated in the table in Figure 9.3. These guidelines make it possible for teachers to give students books to read that they can comprehend and enjoy.

GROUPING CONFIGURATIONS

Students benefit from working in a variety of grouping configurations: small group, whole group, partners, and individual (Morrow et al. 2002). For instance, writing to and for, reading aloud, shared writing, and shared reading are appropriate for whole class or small group settings, while guided writing and guided reading are ideal for small group configurations (see Figure 9.4). Sometimes the small guided groups are determined by achievement, needs, or interests.

TIME

Most students need more time to write and read in school. For some students, the problem is that too little time is allocated for literacy classes. In other settings, the time is allocated but is not used wisely. Many teacher studies on instructional effectiveness have noted that students in an

Whole Class	Small Group	Individual
■ Writing to or for ■ Reading aloud ■ Core books ■ Shared reading and writing ■ Strategy lessons.	■ Shared reading and writing ■ Guided reading and writing ■ Literature circles ■ Strategic needs groups ■ Interest groups ■ Paired reading ■ Readers theatre.	■ Sustained silent reading ■ Independent reading and writing ■ Writers' and readers' workshops.

Figure 9.4: A balance of grouping configurations

exemplary teacher's classroom read and write twice as much than those students in typical teachers' classrooms because:

> Many of the skills involved in writing, such as grammar and spelling, reinforce reading skills, and effective instruction will help students read like writers and write like readers. Students need instruction in the writing process, but they especially need that instruction to be connected to the kinds of writing tasks they will have to perform well in school and beyond. Attention therefore should be given not only to increasing the amount of writing instruction students receive and the amount of writing they do, but also to increasing the quality of writing instruction and assignments (Biancarosa and Snow 2004, 19).

Richard Allington recommends that teachers provide their students 90 minutes daily for actual reading. He notes how students who spend more time reading have much higher achievement (2006). Likewise, researchers find that increased reading time correlates with improved achievement, richer vocabulary growth, and increased reading fluency.

SUMMARY

There is no simplistic formula or commercial program that leads to engaged writers and readers. Indeed, successful teachers can use a number of different teaching styles and materials to achieve thoughtful literacy (Ladson-Billings 1996). Yet, key characteristics exist over and over in classrooms where students become engaged readers and writers.

In this volume, we have chosen one model that we feel allows teachers and students to weave a compelling tapestry of reading and writing. This model emphasizes the need for a literacy-rich environment where students have a balance of choices, challenges, and conversations. Strategies are modeled, taught, and practiced in a scaffolded manner, providing reading and writing to, with, and by students. This model allows for students to learn and work in large groups, small groups, with partners, and independently. Yet, it is the passionate teacher who makes the difference in the reading and writing lives of students in Grade 3 and beyond. We envision classrooms with engaged students and teachers where student achievement is high and student enjoyment of reading and writing abound.

References–
Professional
Materials

Akerson, Valarie L. and Terrell A. Young. 2004. "Nonfiction Know-How: Sure-fire Strategies for Effectively Using Nonfiction Trade Books in Your Science Classroom." *Science & Children*. Volume 41, number 6, March, pages 48–51.

Allington, Richard L. 1977. "If They Don't Read Much, How They Ever Gonna Get Good?" *Journal of Reading*. Volume 21, number 1, pages 57–61.

Allington, Richard L. 2006. *What Really Matters for Struggling Readers: Designing Research-Based Programs,* 2/e. Boston, MA: Allyn and Bacon.

Allington, Richard L. and Patricia M. Cunningham. 2001. *Schools That Work: Where All Children Read and Write,* 2/e. Boston, MA: Allyn and Bacon.

Allington, Richard L. and Peter H. Johnston. 2002. *Reading to Learn: Lessons from Exemplary Fourth-Grade Classrooms.* New York, NY: Guilford Press.

Anderson, Richard C., Elfrieda H. Hiebert, Judith A. Scott, and Ian A. G. Wilkinson. 1985. *Becoming a Nation of Readers: The Report of the Commission on Reading.* Champaign, IL: Center for the Study of Reading.

Anderson, Richard C., Paul T. Wilson, and Linda G. Fielding. 1988. "Growth in Reading and How Children Spend their Time Outside of School." *Reading Research Quarterly*. Volume 23, number 3, Summer, pages 285–303.

Applegate, Anthony and Mary Applegate. 2004. "The Peter Effect: Reading Habits and Attitudes of Preservice Teachers." *The Reading Teacher*. Volume 57, number 4, pages 554–563.

Artley, A. Sterl. 1944. "A Study of Certain Relationships Existing Between General Reading Comprehension and Reading Comprehension in a Specific Subject Matter Area." *Journal of Educational Research*. Volume 37, number 6, pages 464–473.

Beaver, Joetta and Mark Carter. 2004. *Developmental Reading Assessment K-8,* 2/e. Upper Saddle River, NJ: Celebration Press.

Biancarosa, Gina, and Catherine E. Snow. 2004. *Reading Next: A Vision for Action and Research in Middle and High School Literacy: A Report to Carnegie Corporation of New York.* Washington, DC: Alliance for Excellent Education.

Bishop, Rudine Sims and Janet Hickman. 1992. "Four or Fourteen or Forty: Picture Books Are for Everyone." In *Beyond Words: Picture Books for Older Readers and Writers,* edited by Susan Benedict and Lenore Carlisle, 1–10. Portsmouth, NH: Heinemann.

Block, Cathy Collins and Michael Pressley, eds. 2002. *Comprehension Instruction: Research-Based Best Practices.* New York, NY: Guilford Press.

Bond, Guy L., and Robert Dykstra. 1997. "The Cooperative Research Program in First-Grade Reading Instruction." *Reading Research Quarterly.* Volume 32, number 4, pages 348–428.

Bruning, Roger, and Barbara M. Schweiger. 1997. "Integrating Science and Literacy Experiences to Motivate Student Learning." In *Reading Engagement: Motivating Readers through Integrated Instruction*, edited by John T. Guthrie and Allan Wigfield, 149–167. Newark, DE: International Reading Association.

Calkins, Lucy McCormick. 2001. *The Art of Teaching Reading.* New York, NY and Boston, MA: Allyn & Bacon.

Clarke, Shirley. 2003. *Enriching Feedback in the Primary Classroom: Oral and Written Feedback from Teachers and Children.* London: Hodder & Stoughton.

Cunningham, Patricia Marr and Richard L. Allington. 2003. *Classrooms That Work: Where They Can All Read and Write,* 3/e. Boston, MA: Allyn & Bacon.

Daniels, Harvey. 2004. "Building a Classroom Library." *Voices from the Middle.* Volume 11, number 4, May, pages 44–46.

Darling-Hammond, Linda. 2000. Teacher Quality and Student Achievement: A Review of State Policy Evidence. *Educational Policy Analysis Archives.* Volume 8, number 1, pages 1–42.

Duffy, Gerald. 2002. "The Case for Direct Explanation of Strategies." In *Comprehension Instruction: Research-Based Best Practices,* edited by Cathy Collins Block and Michael Pressley, 28–41. New York, NY: Guilford Press.

Ferguson, Ronald F. 1991. "Paying for Public Education: New Evidence on How and Why Money Matters." *Harvard Journal on Legislation.* Volume 28, number 2, pages 465–498.

Fisher, Douglas, James Flood, Diane Lapp, and Nancy Frey. 2004. "Interactive Read-Alouds: Is there a Common Set of Implementation Practices?" *The Reading Teacher.* Volume 58, number 1, pages 8–17.

Fountas, Irene C. and Gay Su Pinnell. 2001. *Guiding Readers and Writers (Grades 3–6): Teaching Comprehension, Genre, and Content Literacy.* Portsmouth, NH: Heinemann.

Fractor, Jan Sorrell, Marjorie Ciruti Woodruff, Miriam G. Martinez, and William H. Teale. 1993. "Let's Not Miss Opportunities to Promote Voluntary Reading: Classroom Libraries in the Elementary School." *The Reading Teacher.* Volume 46, pages 476–484.

Franco, Betsy. 2005. *Conversations with a Poet: Inviting Poetry into K-12 Classrooms.* Katonah, NY: Richard C. Owen Publishers, Inc.

Friedberg, Barbara and Elizabeth Strong. 1989. "Please Don't Stop There!": The Power of Reading Aloud." In *Children's Literature in the Classroom: Weaving Charlotte's Web*, edited by Janet Hickman and Bernice E. Cullinan, 39–48. Needham Heights, MA: Christopher-Gordon Publishers, Inc.

Gambrell, Linda B. and Susan Anders Mazzoni. 1999. "Principles of Best Practice: Finding the Common Ground." In *Best Practice in Literacy Instruction*, edited by Linda B. Gambrell, Lesley Mandel Morrow, Susan B. Neuman, and Michael Pressley, 11–21. New York, NY: Guilford Press.

Gee, James Paul. 1994. "First Language Acquisition as a Guide for Theories of Learning and Pedagogy." *Linguistics and Education*. Volume 6, pages 331–354.

Gee, James Paul. 2004. "Language in the Science Classroom: Academic and Social Languages as the Heart of School Based Literacy." In *Crossing Borders in Literacy and Science Instruction: Perspectives on Theory and Practice*, edited by E. Wendy Saul, 13–22. Newark, DE: International Reading Association.

Giorgis, Cyndi and Nancy J. Johnson. 2005. "Revisiting Read Alouds." *Journal of Children's Literature*. Volume 31, number 1, pages 89–97.

Guthrie, John T. 2004. "Teaching for Literacy Engagement." *Journal of Literacy Research*, Volume 36, Number 1, pages 1–29.

Guthrie, John T., and Nicole M. Humenick. 2004. "Motivating Students to Read: Evidence for Classroom Practices that Increase Reading Motivation and Achievement." In *The Voice of Evidence in Reading Research*, edited by Peggy McCardle and Vinita Chhabra, 329–354. Baltimore, MD: Brookes Publishing.

Guthrie, John T., Schafer, W.D., Von Secker, C., & Alban, T. 2000. "Contributions of integrated reading instruction and text resources to achievement and engagement in a statewide school improvement program." *Journal of Educational Research, 93*, 211–226.

Hadaway, Nancy L., Sylvia M. Vardell., and Terrell A. Young. 2001. "Scaffolding Oral Language Development through Poetry for Students Learning English." *The Reading Teacher*. Volume 54, number 8, pages 796–806.

Hadaway, Nancy L., Sylvia M. Vardell., and Terrell A. Young. 2002. *Literature-Based Instruction with English Language Learners, K-12*. Boston, MA: Allyn & Bacon.

Hadaway, Nancy L., Sylvia M. Vardell, and Terrell A. Young. 2006. "Language Play, Language Work: Using Poetry to Develop Oral Language." In *Supporting the Literacy Development of English Learners: Success in All Classrooms*, edited by Terrell A. Young and Nancy L. Hadaway, 168–184. Newark, DE: International Reading Assocation.

Hahn, Mary Lee. 2002. *Reconsidering Read-Aloud*. Portland, ME: Stenhouse.

Halliday, Michael A. K. and Ruqaiya Hasan. 1985. *Language, Context and Text: A Social Semiotic Perspective*. Geelong, Victoria, AU: Deakin University Press.

Harvey, Stephanie and Anne Goudvis. 2000. *Strategies That Work: Teaching Comprehension to Enhance Understanding.* Portland, ME: Stenhouse.

Harwayne, Shelley. 1999. *Going Public: Priorities and Practice at the Manhattan New School.* Portsmouth, NH: Heinemann.

Hoffman, James, Nancy Roser, and Jennifer Battle. 1993. "Reading Aloud in Classrooms: From the Modal toward a 'Model.'" *The Reading Teacher.* Volume 46, number 6, pages 496–503.

Hoyt, Linda, Margaret Mooney, and Brenda Parkes. 2003. *Exploring Informational Texts: From Theory to Practice.* Portsmouth, NH: Heinemann.

Hsueh-Chao, Marcella Hu and Paul Nation. 2000. "Unknown Vocabulary Density and Reading Comprehension." *Reading in a Foreign Language.* Volume 13, number 1, pages 403–430.

Jones, Patrick. 2001. "Books for Struggling and Reluctant Readers." *Voices from the Middle.* Volume 9, number 2, December, 67–70.

Keene, Ellin Oliver and Suzanne Zimmermann. 1997. *Mosaic of Thought: Teaching Comprehension in a Reader's Workshop.* Portsmouth, NH: Heinemann.

Ketch, Ann. 2005. "Conversation: The Comprehension Connection." *The Reading Teacher.* Volume 59, number 1, pages 8–13.

Krashen. Stephen D. 2004. *The Power of Reading: Insights from the Research,* 2/e. Portsmouth, NH: Heinemann.

Ladson-Billings, Gloria. 1996. *The Dreamkeepers: Successful Teachers of African American Children.* San Francisco, CA: Jossey-Bass.

Leslie, Lauren and JoAnne Caldwell. 2001. *Qualitative Reading Inventory-3,* 3/e. Boston, MA: Allyn & Bacon.

McClure, Amy with Peggy Harrison and Sheryl Reed. 1990. *Sunrises and Songs: Reading and Writing Poetry in an Elementary Classroom.* Portsmouth, NH: Heinemann.

Miller, Debbie. 2002. *Reading with Meaning: Teaching Comprehension in the Primary Grades.* Portland, ME: Stenhouse.

Ministry of Education. 1985. *Reading in Junior Classes.* Wellington, New Zealand: Learning Media.

Ministry of Education. 1992. *Dancing with the Pen: The Learner as a Writer.* Wellington, New Zealand: Learning Media.

Ministry of Education. 1993. *New Zealand Curriculum Framework.* Wellington, New Zealand: Learning Media.

Ministry of Education. 1997. *Reading for Life: The Learner as a Reader.* Wellington, New Zealand: Learning Media.

Ministry of Education. 2003. *Quality Teaching for Diverse Students in Schooling: Best Evidence Synthesis.* Wellington, New Zealand: Ministry of Education.

Mooney, Margaret E. 1988. *Developing Life-long Readers.* Wellington, New Zealand: Ministry of Education.

Mooney, Margaret E. 1990. *Reading To, With, and By Children.* Katonah, NY: Richard C. Owen Publishers, Inc.

Mooney, Margaret E. 2001. *Text Forms and Features: A Resource for Intentional Teaching.* Katonah, NY: Richard C. Owen Publishers, Inc.

Mooney, Margaret E. 2004. *A Book Is a Present: Selecting Text for Intentional Teaching.* Katonah, NY: Richard C. Owen Publishers, Inc.

Mooney, Margaret E. 2005. "Characteristics of Learners." In *Learning in the Content Areas: The Role of Literacy.* Katonah, NY: Richard C. Owen Publishers, Inc.

Morgan, Bruce with Deb Odom. 2005. *Writing through the Tween Years: Supporting Writers, Grades 3–6.* Portland, ME: Stenhouse.

Morrison, Timothy G., James S. Jacobs, and William R. Swinyard. 1999. "Do Teachers Who Read Personally Use Recommended Literacy Practices in Their Classrooms?" *Reading Research and Instruction.* Volume 38, number 2, pages 81–100.

Morrow, Leslie Mandel. 2003. "Motivating Lifelong Voluntary Readers." In *Handbook of Research on Teaching the English Language Arts*, edited by James Flood, Diane Lapp, James R. Squires, and Julie M. Jensen, 857–867. Mahwah, NJ: Lawrence Erlbaum Associates.

Morrow, Leslie Mandel, Gregory Wamsley, Kimberly Duhammel, and Nancy Fittipaldi. 2002. "A Case Study of Exemplary Practice in Fourth Grade." In *Teaching Reading: Effective Schools, Accomplished Teachers,* edited by Barbara M. Taylor and P. David Pearson, 289–307. Mahwah, NJ: Lawrence Erlbaum Associates.

Moss, Barbara. 2002. *Exploring the Literature of Fact: Children's Nonfiction Trade Books in the Elementary Classroom.* New York, NY: Guilford Press.

Nagy, William and Richard C. Anderson. 1984. "How Many Words Are There in Printed School English?" *Reading Research Quarterly.* Volume 19, number 3, pages 304–330.

National Institute of Child Health and Human Development. 2000. Report of the National Reading Panel. Teaching children to read: An evidence-based assessment of the scientific research literature on reading and its implications for reading instruction (NIH Publication No. 00–4769). Washington, DC: U.S. Government Printing Office.

Neuman, Susan B. 1999. "Books Make a Difference: A Study of Access to Literacy." *Reading Research Quarterly.* Volume 34, number 3, pages 286–311.

Oczkus, Lori D. 2003. *Reciprocal Teaching at Work: Strategies for Improving Reading Comprehension.* Newark, DE: International Reading Association.

Oczkus, Lori D. 2004. *Super Six Comprehension Strategies: 35 Lessons and More for Reading Success.* Norwood, MA: Christopher-Gordon Publishers, Inc.

Palincsar, Annemarie S. and Ann L. Brown. 1984. "Reciprocal Teaching of Comprehension-Fostering and Comprehension-Monitoring Activities." *Cognition and Instruction.* Volume 2, number 2, pages 117–175.

Parkes, Brenda. 2000. *Read It Again! Revisiting Shared Reading.* Portland, ME: Stenhouse.

Pearson, P. David and Margaret C. Gallagher. 1983. "The Instruction of Reading Comprehension." *Contemporary Educational Psychology.* Volume 8, pages 317–344.

Pratt, Harold and Norby Pratt. 2004. "Integrating Science and Literacy Instruction With a Common Goal of Learning Science Content." In *Crossing Borders in Literacy and Science Instruction: Perspectives on Theory and Practice,* edited by E. Wendy Saul, 395–405. Newark, DE: International Reading Association.

Pressley, Michael. 2002. *Reading Instruction That Works: The Case for Balanced Teaching,* 2/e. New York: Guilford Press.

Reading Lady, The website. http://www.readinglady.com/mosaic/tools/tools.htm.

Routman, Regie. 1999. *Conversations: Strategies for Teaching, Learning, and Evaluating.* Portsmouth, NH: Heinemann.

Routman, Regie. 2003. *Reading Essentials: The Specifics You Need to Teach Reading Well.* Portsmouth, NH: Heinemann.

Routman, Regie. 2005. *Writing Essentials: Raising Expectations and Results While Simplifying Teaching.* Portsmouth, NH: Heinemann.

Samway, Katharine Davies and Gail Whang. 1995. *Literature Study Circles in a Multicultural Classroom.* York, ME: Stenhouse.

Saul, E. Wendy, ed. 2004. *Crossing Borders in Literacy and Science Education: Perspectives on Theory and Practice.* Newark, DE: International Reading Association.

Schlick Noe, Katherine L. and Nancy J. Johnson. 1999. *Getting Started with Literature Circles.* Norwood, MA: Christopher-Gordon Publishers, Inc.

Serafini, Frank and Cyndi Giorgis. 2003. *Reading Aloud and Beyond: Fostering the Intellectual Life with Older Readers.* Portsmouth, NH: Heinemann.

Sibberson, Franki and Karen Szymusiak. 2003. *Still Learning to Read: Teaching Students in Grades 3–6.* Portland, ME: Stenhouse.

Smith, John W. A. and Warwick B. Elley. 1997. *How Children Learn to Read.* Katonah, NY: Richard C. Owen Publishers, Inc.

Smith, Michael W. and Jeffrey D. Wilhelm. 2002. *"Reading Don't Fix No Chevys": Literacy in the Lives of Young Men.* Portsmouth, NH: Heinemann.

Snow, Catherine E., chair. 2002. *Reading for Understanding: Toward a Research and Development Program in Reading Comprehension.* Published for Office of Educational Research and Improvement, U.S. Department of Education. Pittsburgh, PA: RAND.

Stahl, Steven A. 1999. *Vocabulary Development.* Cambridge, MA: Brookline Books.

Stahl, Steven A. 2004. "What Do We Know About Fluency?" In *The Voice of Evidence in Reading Research,* edited by Peggy McCardle and Vinita Chhabra, 187–211. Baltimore, MD: Brookes Publishing.

Stanovich, Keith E. 1986. "Matthew Effects in Reading: Some Consequences of Individual Differences in the Acquisition of Literacy." *Reading Research Quarterly.* Volume 21, number 4, pages 360–407.

Stead, Tony. 2001. *Is That a Fact? Teaching Nonfiction Writing K-3.* York, ME: Stenhouse.

Stoodt-Hill, Barbara D. and Linda B. Amspaugh-Corson. 2005. *Children's Literature: Discovery for a Lifetime,* 3/e. Upper Saddle River, NJ: Prentice Hall.

Taylor, Barbara M., Barbara J. Frye, and Geoffrey M. Maruyama. 1990. "Time Spent Reading and Reading Growth." *American Educational Research Journal.* Volume 27, number 2, pages 351–362.

Taylor, Barbara M., Michael Pressley, and P. David Pearson. 2002. "Increasing Reading Achievement: Research-Supported Characteristics of Teachers and Schools." In *Teaching Reading: Effective Schools, Accomplished Teachers,* edited by Barbara M. Taylor and P. David Pearson, 361–387. Mahwah, NJ: Lawrence Erlbaum Associates.

Thier, Marlene and Bennett Daviss. 2002. *The New Science Literacy: Using Language Skills to Help Students Learn Science.* Portsmouth, NH: Heinemann.

Tovani, Cris. 2000. *I Read It, But I Don't Get It.* Portland, ME: Stenhouse.

Trelease, Jim. 2001. *The Read-Aloud Handbook.* New York, NY: Penguin.

Vardell, Sylvia M. 2003. "Using Read Aloud to Explore the Layers of Nonfiction." In *Making Facts Come Alive: Choosing and Using Nonfiction Literature K-8,* 2/e, edited by Rosemary A. Bamford and Janice V. Kristo, 192–207. Norwood, MA: Christopher-Gordon Publishers, Inc.

Webster, Joan Parker. n.d. *Learning to Question the Word and the World: Exploring Critical Literacies in the Classroom.* Katonah, NY: Richard C. Owen Publishers, Inc., forthcoming.

Wells, Gordon. 1999. *Dialogic Inquiry: Toward a Sociocultural Practice and Theory of Education.* New York, NY: Cambridge University Press.

Worthy, Jo, Karen Broaddus, and Gay Ivey. 2001. *Pathways to Independence: Reading, Writing, and Learning in Grades 3–8.* New York, NY: Guilford Press.

Worthy, Jo, Megan Moorman, and Margo Turner. 1999. "What Johnny Likes to Read Is Hard to Find in School." *Reading Research Quarterly.* Volume 34, number 1, pages 12–27.

Young, Terrell A., Barbara Moss, and Linda Cornwell. n.d. "Classroom Libraries: A Place for Nonfiction and Nonfiction In Its Place." Forthcoming.

Young, Terrell A. and Sylvia M. Vardell. 1993. "Weaving Readers Theatre and Nonfiction into the Curriculum." *The Reading Teacher.* Volume 46, number 5, pages 396–406.

References–
Children's Books

Adler, David. 2001. *A Picture Book of Sacagawea*. New York, NY: Holiday House.

Adler, David. 2003. *A Picture Book of Lewis and Clark*. New York, NY: Holiday House.

Armstrong, Jennifer. 1998. *Shipwreck at the Bottom of the World: The Extraordinary True Story of Shackleton and the* Endurance. New York, NY: Crown.

Blumberg, Rhoda. 1987. *The Incredible Journey of Lewis and Clark*. New York: Lothrop, Lee and Shepard.

Blumberg, Rhoda. 1998. *What's the Deal? Jefferson, Napoleon, and the Louisiana Purchase*. Washington, DC: National Geographic.

Blumberg, Rhoda. 2004. *York's Adventures with Lewis and Clark: An African-American's Part in the Great Expedition*. New York, NY: HarperCollins.

Bruchac, Joseph. 1994. *A Boy Called Slow: The True Story of Sitting Bull*. New York, NY: Philomel.

Bruchac, Joseph. 1999. *Seeing the Circle*. Katonah, NY: Richard C. Owen Publishers, Inc.

Bunting, Eve. *Jin Woo*. 2001. New York, NY: Houghton Mifflin/Clarion.

Burleigh, Robert. 1998. *Black Whiteness: Admiral Byrd Alone in the Antarctic*. New York, NY: Atheneum.

Byrd, Robert. 2003. *Leonardo: Beautiful Dreamer*. New York, NY: Dutton.

Caisley, Raewyn. 1997. *Raewyn's Got the Writing Bug*. Santa Rosa, CA: SRA/Voyages.

Carlson, Lori Marie, editor. 2005. *Red Hot Salsa: Bilingual Poems on Being Young and Latino in the United States*. New York, NY: Henry Holt.

Choi, Yangsook. 2001. *The Name Jar*. New York, NY: Random House Children's Books.

Clarke, Penny. 2002. *Sharks*. New York, NY: Franklin Watts.

Codell, Esmé Raji. 2004. *Sing a Song of Tuna Fish: Hard-to-Swallow Stories from Fifth Grade*. New York, NY: Hyperion Books for Children.

Colfer, Eoin. 2001. *Artemis Fowl*. New York, NY: Hyperion.

Colfer, Eoin. 2002. *The Arctic Incident*. New York, NY: Hyperion.

Colfer, Eoin. 2003. *The Eternity Code*. New York, NY: Hyperion.

Colfer, Eoin. 2004. *The Artemis Fowl Files: The Ultimate Guide to the Best-Selling Series.* New York, NY: Hyperion.

Colfer, Eoin. 2005. *The Opal Deception.* New York, NY: Hyperion.

Collier, James Lincoln. 2003. *The Sitting Bull You Never Knew.* New York, NY: Children's Press.

Cosson, M. J. 1999. *The Mystery of Ben Franklin's Ghost.* Logan, IA: Perfection Learning.

Creech, Sharon. 1994. *Walk Two Moons.* New York, NY: HarperCollins Children's Books.

Crowe, Chris. 2002. *Mississippi Trial, 1955.* New York, NY: Phyllis Fogelman Books.

Crowe, Chris. 2003. *Getting Away with Murder: The True Story of the Emmett Till Case.* New York, NY: Dial/Penguin.

Currie, S. 2004. *All About Potatoes.* New York, NY: Newbridge Educational Publishing.

DiCamillo, Kate. 2001. *Because of Winn-Dixie.* Cambridge, MA: Candlewick Press.

DiCamillo, Kate. 2003. *The Tale of Despereaux: Being the Story of a Mouse, a Princess, Some Soup, and a Spool of Thread.* Cambridge, MA: Candlewick Press.

Dotlich, Rebecca Kai. 2001. *When Riddles Come Rumbling: Poems to Ponder.* Honesdale, PA: Wordsong/Boyds Mills Press.

Erdrich, Liselotte. 2003. *Sacagawea.* Minneapolis, MN: Carolrhoda.

Fletcher, Ralph. 1995. *Fig Pudding.* New York, NY: Houghton Mifflin/Clarion.

Fletcher, Ralph. 2005. *A Writing Kind of Day: Poems for Young Poets.* Honesdale, PA: Wordsong/Boyds Mills Press.

Florian, Douglas. 1998. *Insectlopedia.* San Diego, CA: Harcourt.

Florian, Douglas. 2000. *Mammalabilia.* San Diego, CA: Harcourt.

Freedman, Russell. 1987. *Indian Chiefs.* New York, NY: Holiday House.

Freedman, Russell. 1987. *Lincoln: A Photobiography.* New York, NY: Clarion.

Freedman, Russell. 1988. *Buffalo Hunt.* New York, NY: Holiday House.

Freedman, Russell. 1990. *Franklin Delano Roosevelt.* New York, NY: Clarion.

Gallo, Donald R., editor. 2005. *First Crossing: Stories about Teen Immigrants.* Cambridge, MA: Candlewick Press.

Gibbons, Gail. 2005. *Owls.* New York, NY: Holiday House.

Gold, Alison Leslie. 2000. *A Special Fate: Chiune Sugihara, Hero of the Holocaust.* New York, NY: Scholastic.

Gollub, Matthew. 1998. *Cool Melons—Turn to Frogs! The Life and Poems of Issa.* New York, NY: Lee & Low.

Graham, Joan Bransfield. 1994. *Splish Splash.* Boston, MA: Houghton Mifflin.

Graham, Joan Bransfield. 1999. *Flicker Flash.* Boston, MA: Houghton Mifflin.

Halls, Kelly Milner. 2003. *Dinosaur Mummies: Beyond Bare-bone Fossils.* Plain City, OH: Darby Creek Publishing.

CAUGHT IN THE SPELL OF WRITING AND READING

Harley, Avis. 2000. *Fly with Poetry: An ABC of Poetry*. Honesdale, PA: Wordsong/Boyds Mills Press.

Heard, Georgia. 1992. *Creatures of Earth, Sea, and Sky: Animal Poems*. Honesdale, PA: Wordsong/Boyds Mills Press.

Hopkins, Lee Bennett, editor. 2000. *My America: A Poetry Atlas of the United States*. New York, NY: Simon & Schuster.

Hopkinson, Deborah. 2003. *Shutting out the Sky: Life in the Tenements of New York 1880–1924*. New York, NY: Orchard Books.

Hort, Leonard. 2002. *Ring of Fire*. New York, NY: Newbridge Educational Publishing.

Hoyt-Goldsmith, Diane. 2001. *Celebrating Ramadan*. New York, NY: Holiday House.

InfoQuest. 2003. Austin, TX: Rigby.

Janeczko, Paul B. 2001. *A Poke in the I: A Collection of Concrete Poems*. Cambridge, MA: Candlewick Press.

Janeczko, Paul B. 2005. *A Kick in the Head: An Everyday Guide to Poetic Forms*. Cambridge, MA: Candlewick Press.

Kadohata, Cynthia. 2004. *Kira-Kira*. New York, NY: Atheneum.

Katz, Bobbi. 2000. *We the People*. New York, NY: HarperCollins/Greenwillow.

Kramer, Stephen. 2001. *Hidden Worlds: Looking through a Scientist's Microscope*. Boston, MA: Houghton Mifflin.

Krull, Kathleen. 1998. *Lives of the Presidents: Fame, Shame (and What the Neighbors Thought)*. San Diego, CA: Harcourt Brace.

Lewis, J. Patrick. 2005. *Heroes and She-roes: Poems of Amazing and Everyday Heroes*. New York, NY: Penguin USA/Dial Books for Young Readers.

Lewis, J. Patrick. 2005. *Monumental Verses*. Washington, DC: National Geographic Children's Book.

London, Jonathan. 2000. *Panther: Shadow of the Swamp* Cambridge, MA: Candlewick Press.

Lowry, Lois. 1993. *The Giver*. Boston, MA: Houghton Mifflin.

Lunis, Natalie and Nancy White. 2000. *Exploring Everyday Wonders*. New York, NY: Newbridge Educational Publishing.

Markle, Sandra. 2005. *Outside and Inside Mummies*. New York, NY: Walker Books for Young Readers.

Marrin, Albert. 2004. *Old Hickory: Andrew Jackson and the American People*. New York, NY: Dutton.

McNaughton, Colin. 2000. *Wish You Were Here (and I Wasn't): Poems and Pictures for Globe Trotters*. Cambridge, MA: Candlewick Press.

Mochizuki, Ken. 1997. *Passage to Freedom: The Sugihara Story*. New York, NY: Lee & Low Books.

Montgomery, Sy. 1999. *The Snake Scientist*. Boston, MA: Houghton Mifflin.

Montgomery, Sy. 2001. *The Man-Eating Tigers of Sundarbans*. Boston, MA: Houghton Mifflin.

Mora, Pat. 2000. *My Own True Name: New and Selected Poems for Young Adults: 1984–1999*. Houston, TX: Piñata Books.

Morley, Jacqueline. 1998. *Across America: The Story of Lewis and Clark*. Danbury, CT: Franklin Watts.

Murphy, Claire Rudolph. 2005. *I Am Sacagawea, I Am York: Our Journey West with Lewis and Clark*. New York, NY: Walker Books for Young Readers.

Murphy, Jim. 1995. *The Great Fire*. New York, NY: Scholastic.

Nimmo, Jenny. 2002. *Midnight for Charlie Bone*. New York, NY: Orchard Books.

Nimmo, Jenny. 2003. *Charlie Bone and the Time Twister*. New York, NY: Orchard Books.

Nimmo, Jenny. 2004. *Charlie Bone and the Invisible Boy*. New York, NY: Orchard Books.

Nimmo, Jenny. 2005. *Charlie Bone and the Castle of Mirrors*. New York, NY: Orchard Books.

Nye, Naomi Shihab. 2005. *A Maze Me: Poems for Girls*. New York, NY: Greenwillow.

Parkes, Brenda. 2001. *The Wolf's Story*. Austin, TX: Rigby.

Patent, Dorothy Hinshaw. 2002. *Animals on the Trail with Lewis and Clark*. New York, NY: Clarion/Houghton Mifflin.

Patent, Dorothy Hinshaw. 2003. *Plants on the Trail with Lewis and Clark*. New York, NY: Clarion/Houghton Mifflin.

Peck, Richard. 1998. *A Long Way from Chicago: A Novel in Stories*. New York, NY: Dial Books for Young Readers.

Peck, Richard. 2000. *A Year Down Yonder*. New York, NY: Dial Books for Young Readers.

Prelutsky, Jack. 2000. *It's Raining Pigs & Noodles*. New York, NY: HarperCollins.

Prelutsky, Jack. 2004. *If Not for the Cat*. New York, NY: Greenwillow.

Prelutsky, Jack. 2005. *Read a Rhyme, Write a Rhyme*. New York, NY: Alfred A. Knopf.

Pringle, Laurence. 1997. *Nature! Wild and Wonderful*. Katonah, NY: Richard C. Owen Publishers, Inc.

Ranger Rick Science. 2004. New York, NY: Newbridge Educational Publishing.

Rappaport, Doreen. 2005. *The School Is Not White! A True Story of the Civil Rights Movement*. New York, NY: Hyperion Books.

Read to Learn Social Studies. 2005. New York, NY: Newbridge Educational Publishing.

Ride, Sally and Tam O'Shaughnessy. 1999. *The Mystery of Mars*. New York, NY: Crown Books for Young Readers.

Riordan, Rick. 2005. *The Lightning Thief*. New York, NY: Hyperion.

Riordan, Rick. 2006. *The Sea of Monsters*. New York, NY: Hyperion/Miramax.

CAUGHT IN THE SPELL OF **WRITING AND READING**

Rowling, J. K. 1997. *Harry Potter and the Sorcerer's Stone*. New York, NY: Arthur A. Levine/Scholastic.

Rowling, J. K. 1999. *Harry Potter and the Chamber of Secrets*. New York, NY: Arthur A. Levine/Scholastic.

Rowling, J. K. 1999. *Harry Potter and the Prisoner of Azkaban*. New York, NY: Arthur A. Levine/Scholastic.

Rowling, J. K. 2000. *Harry Potter and the Goblet of Fire*. New York, NY: Arthur A. Levine/Scholastic.

Rowling, J. K. 2003. *Harry Potter and the Order of the Phoenix*. New York, NY: Arthur A. Levine/Scholastic.

Rowling, J. K. 2005. *Harry Potter and the Half-Blood Prince*. New York, NY: Arthur A. Levine/Scholastic.

Rylant, Cynthia. 2005. *Boris*. San Diego, CA: Harcourt Children's Books.

Santella, Andrew. 2001. *Lewis and Clark*. New York, NY: Franklin Watts.

Say, Allen. 1999. *Tea with Milk*. New York, NY: Houghton Mifflin.

Schanzer, Rosalyn. 2002. *How We Crossed the West: The Adventures of Lewis and Clark*. Washington, DC: National Geographic.

Scieszka, Jon, editor. 2005. *Guys Write for Guys Read*. New York, NY: Penguin/Viking.

Seinfeld, Jerry. 2002. *Halloween*. New York, NY: Little, Brown & Co.

Sidman, Joyce. 2005. *Song of the Water Boatman & Other Pond Poems*. New York, NY: Houghton Mifflin.

Siebert, Diane. 1989. *Heartland*. New York, NY: HarperCollins.

Siebert, Diane. 2006. *Tour America: A Journey through Poems and Arts*. San Francisco, CA: Chronicle Books.

Silverstein, Shel. 1981. *A Light in the Attic*. New York, NY: HarperCollins.

Sneve, Virginia Driving Hawk. 2005. *Bad River Boys: A Meeting of the Lakota Sioux with Lewis and Clark*. New York, NY: Holiday House.

Soto, Gary. 2005. *Worlds Apart: Traveling with Fernie and Me*. New York, NY: Penguin/Putnam Juvenile.

Stanley, Diane. 1996. *Leonardo da Vinci*. New York, NY: HarperCollins.

Stanley, Jerry. 1992. *Children of the Dust Bowl: The True Story of the School at Weedpatch Camp*. New York, NY: Random House/Crown Books for Young Readers.

Stein, R. Conrad. 1997. *Lewis and Clark*. New York, NY: Grolier/Children's Press.

Stroud, Jonathan. 2003. *The Amulet of Samarkand*. New York, NY: Hyperion.

Stroud, Jonathan. 2004. *The Golem's Eye*. New York, NY: Hyperion.

Stroud, Jonathan. 2005. *Ptolemy's Gate*. New York, NY: Hyperion/Miramax.

Sullivan, George. 1999. *Lewis and Clark (In Their Own Words)*. New York, NY: Scholastic Reference.

Swanson, Diane. 1994. *Safari Beneath the Sea: The Wonder World of the North Pacific Coast*. San Francisco, CA: Sierra Club.

Taylor, Mildred D. 1976. *Roll of Thunder, Hear My Cry*. New York, NY: Dial Books for Young Readers.

U'Ren, Andrea. 2003. *Mary Smith*. New York, NY: Farrar, Straus and Giroux.

Weatherford, Carole Boston. 2004. *Freedom on the Menu: The Greensboro Sit-Ins*. New York, NY: Dial Books for Young Readers.

Wilcox, Charlotte. 1993. *Mummies and Their Mysteries*. Minneapolis, MN: Carolrhoda.

Wong, Janet S. 2002. *You Have to Write*. New York, NY: Margaret K. McElderry Books.

Woodruff, Elvira. 1999. *The Memory Coat*. New York, NY: Scholastic Press.

Yolen, Jane. 2002. *Wild Wings: Poems for Young People*. Honesdale, PA: Wordsong/Boyds Mills Press.

Yolen, Jane. 2003. *Least Things: Poems About Small Natures*. Honesdale, PA: Wordsong/Boyds Mills Press.

Index